"A book that made me war~~~~~~~~~~~~~~ with kids. A book that I'll r~~~~~~~~~~ kids. And any adult with an inner child will like it, too.
 John Lee, author of *The Flying Boy, Healing the Wounded Man*

"I found this book to contain valuable insights for parents in recovery. It reviews basic parenting skills and helps parents to focus upon critical issues of breaking the cycle of family codependency."
 Terence T. Gorski, author of
 Passages Through Recovery
 President, The Cenaps Corporation
 The Center for Applied Sciences

"*My Child, My Teacher, My Friend* take us on a deeply personal journey into the realm of parenting. Here we are given permission for our humanness as we learn to care for our children and care for ourselves. A beautifully written and felt book."
 Patricia O'Gorman, Ph.D.
 co-author with Philip Oliver-Diaz, M.S.W.
 Self-Parenting 12 Step Workbook: Windows to Your Inner Child

"Dwight's new book, *My Child, My Teacher, My Friend: One Man's View of Parenting in Recovery*, is his best work yet. Sensitive and easy to read, *My Child* offers terse teaching vignettes about his relationship with his daughter, himself and his parents. It offers guidance to those of us who have taken on the challenge of reparenting ourselves, and hope to those who question their own ability to parent a child."
 Julie Bowden, author, *Recovery: A Guide to Adult Children of Alcoholics* and *Genesis: Spirituality in Recovery from Childhood Traumas*

"I am a parent, and this book touched both my heart and my funny bone."
 Bob Earll, author of *I Got Tired of Pretending: How an Adult Raised in an Alcoholic/Dysfunctional Family Finds Freedom*

"Lovingly written and profoundly touching, Dwight Wolter has written a handbook for the heart."
 F. Forrester Church, minister,
 Unitarian Church of All Souls, New York City;
 Chicago Tribune columnist;
 author of *Everyday Miracles: Stories from Life*

Other Books by Dwight Lee Wolter

A Life Worth Waiting For! For All Adult Children from Dysfunctional Families: Messages from a Survivor (CompCare Publishers, Minneapolis).

"This material was extremely moving. It made me laugh and then cry. I enthusiastically endorse his work."
>John Bradshaw, author,
>*Bradshaw on: The Family* and
>*Healing the Shame that Binds You*

"Vividly and powerfully describes growing up in a dysfunctional family. More significantly, he shares the processes, feelings, and rewards of recovery."
>Sharon Wegscheider-Cruse, lecturer;
>president, Onsite Training and Consulting; founding board chairperson, National Association for Children of Alcoholics (NACoA);
>author, *Another Chance* and *Choicemaking*

Forgiving Our Parents For Adult Children from Dysfunctional Families (CompCare Publishers, Minneapolis)

"Wolter is a trail guide to what's ahead in this area of recovery. We could all use a friend in recovery with this much thoughtfulness and perception."
>*Sober Times,* San Diego

"We are led through his honest and gut-wrenching process of understanding and forgiving his parents. As we experience his personal story, we learn much about ourselves along the way."
>Patricia O'Gorman, Ph.D.,
>Philip Oliver-Diaz, M.S.W.,
>authors of *Breaking the Cycle of Addiction*
>and *12 Steps to Self-Parenting*

My Child, My Teacher, My Friend

One Man's View of Parenting in Recovery

Dwight Lee Wolter

CompCare® Publishers
Minneapolis, Minnesota

©1991 by Dwight Lee Wolter
All rights reserved.
Published in the United States
by CompCare Publishers.

Reproduction in whole or part, in any form, including storage in memory device systems, is forbidden without written permission, except that portions may be used in broadcast or printed commentary or review when attributed fully to author and publication by names.

Library of Congress Cataloging-in-Publication Data
Wolter, Dwight Lee.
    My child, my teacher, my friend: One man's view of parenting in recovery / Dwight Lee Wolter
      p. cm.
      ISBN 0-89638-233-8
       1. Single parents—United States.   2. Fathers and daughters—United States.   3. Adult children of dysfunctional families—United States.   I. Title.
HQ759.915.W65 1991   90-19974
306.85'6—dc20   CIP

Cover and interior design by MacLean and Tuminelly

Inquiries, orders, and catalog requests should be addressed to
CompCare Publishers
2415 Annapolis Lane
Minneapolis, MN 55441
Call toll free 800/328-3330
(Minnesota residents 612/559-4800)

5 4 3 2 1
95 94 93 92 91

To Celeste Sophia Wolter

Contents

I Regret Nothing 1
The Rabbit Died 4
Are Kids Beautiful? 6
What Do You Believe In? 7
It's My Body 8
The Nut with the Umbrella 9
Whose Homework Is This? 11
Intuition 12
Milk Money 13
Just One Wish 16
X-Ray 17
Strawberries 20
Fight Fair 22
Picture Perfect 24
Unlimited Combinations 25
Parenting Myself and My Daughter 26
Act as If 30
Doing It Backwards Is Right 31
Transition 33
All That Is Left 35
The Last Day of School 36
I Want What I Want When I Want It 38
Are My Feelings Okay with You? 42
Birds and Bees 44
Dinosaur Diarrhea 45
Asthma Attack 47
This Is a Test 49
Kids and Money 51
Just Say Yes 53
The Hope of Good Cape 61
Please Tell Me What I'm Feeling 67

Forced Labor   69
No Guarantee   70
Troubleshooter   72
That Daring Young Man on the Flying
Trapeze   74
Coming Home to You   79
Can You Hear the Ocean?   85
A Beautiful Day to Torment a Child   87
Single Parent Nightmare   93
Sick Kid   95
A Grieving Child with a Grieving Child   97
Squeaker's Funeral   106
Burial at Sea   109
Squeaker's Grave Revisited   111
Spooky   112
Pervert or Not?   113
Forgiveness and Children   116
Yikes! The Dentist!   124
Money Where Your Mouth Is   127
Is Santa Dead?   130
Christmas with and without Andrea   134
I'll Blow Your House Down   137
The Mugging   146
Woman without Child   150
Need   152
First Things First   153
God and My Daughter   154
Asset or Liability?   158
Blessed with Addiction   160
A Sense of Self   162
Happy Mother's Day to Me   165
Fruitcake   167
Check the Spelling   168
Hiccups   169

What It Takes   172
Celestial   173
Share Me   174
Parenting in Recovery   176

About the Author   179
Resource List of Topics   181

Mentors, Spies, and Angels

Several people helped me in the writing of this book. Many don't even know they did. This is a partial list of those special people to whom I would like to extend my gratitude: Jane Thomas Noland; Amy Church; Howard Stringer; Chris Kirk; Melva Peterson; Terri Driscoll; Zoe, George, and Bernice Pappas; Bob Morris; Tony Allen; Bob Earll; Sandy Eggers; Patricia Powell; John Buehrens; Charles E. and Winifred M. Wolter; Kris Perry; Jamie Waller; Randie Levine, and the folks at the M.O.C., and, as always, for now and forever, John Lennon.

I Regret Nothing

On a little plaque at the end of a hallway in my apartment is a quote from the French singer Edith Piaf. It says:

"I regret nothing."

I regret nothing because it has taken every moment of my life to get me to where I am today. I have lived a very lovely and also a very painful life. I feel blessed, and yet I wouldn't wish the troubles I have survived on my worst enemy. I appreciate my life much more than I believe I would have, had I not gone through the experience of pain. There is nothing like putting your head on the lap of death to spark a desire to live. I have returned from the land of the dead with fire in my veins. In the past eight years, I have faced everything I had hidden from in the thirty years that preceded them. I have talked and written honestly and publicly about the very things I was once ashamed of. The pain and fear has been immense, as has been the joy and gratitude. It has all been worth it.

My nine-year-old daughter doesn't believe this, of course. Occasionally she walks down the hallway and gazes up at the plaque that says "I regret nothing" and mutters, just loud enough for me to hear, "I don't believe it."

I must confess, she is right, at least about two things:

I regret that I have had to raise Celeste as a single father. In my humble opinion, I have done a wonderful job. I am aware that, if it had not been for my divorce several years ago, I might have remained in a more passive role, earning money while allowing her mother to do most of the parenting. My divorce and my dedication to being a good parent have made me a better father and a better man, but it has been lonely.

I was brought up in a family numbed and broken by addiction. And I have not been able to provide a sense of family for my daughter. I often wonder how it might have felt to have a wife for me and a mother for my daughter, with all of us living under one roof, sharing this mystical journey. I regret that I may never know.

Once upon a time it was impossible for me to imagine being a parent. Now it is impossible for me to imagine not being one. Maybe, someday, there will be a chance to parent again, this time within a family.

I have one more regret. I regret that I will never know what it is like to be pregnant, and to give birth to a child. I was present when my daughter was born. I got as close as I could. I was the first person my daughter saw, and I am very proud of that. But it is not the same.

Someday men may be able to carry the fetus for the entire period of gestation. I have no idea what will happen then. Others say it will mark the beginning of a new reverence for life and children. Others say it will stabilize the work force and finally provide the impetus for adequate day care, maternity benefits, and health insurance.

In any case, the days of parenting being a matter of gender are coming to a close. Many men are becoming more aware of the injustice of women carrying the burden of child care. Many men are becoming aware that by not taking a more active role in their children's upbringing they are missing out on not only the burdens, but the blessings of parenting.

I guess my simple regrets all surround a wish to be more of a father more of the time. Those are sweet regrets. My task today is to accept myself for who and what I am and to love myself for doing the best I can.

It was a rare combination of circumstance, guilt, and love that propelled me into an extremely expensive, three-year struggle for joint custody. Five years ago, after my divorce, once the fanfare and the glory of being a single father wore off, I settled down into the day-to-day routine of loving and raising a three-foot-high little person who thought I was the answer. I have tried to guide her inward to herself, and then outward to the world.

The world divides sharply along the lines of those who are parents and those who are not. I am extremely grateful that, by fate's design, I stand on this side of that line. I had never thought of being a father when Celeste's mother announced her pregnancy. I didn't know if I could do it. But I'm doing just fine.

Parenting Celeste has been the most difficult thing I have ever done. It has also been the most rewarding.

The Rabbit Died

In 1980 my new wife and I took a train on Thanksgiving Day from New Orleans to New York City. We were carrying four suitcases, two turkey sandwiches, and a child in my wife's belly that we didn't know about. We had no jobs, no apartment, little money, but lots of hope. We also had a lot of foolishness and dumb luck, which were more valuable than we could ever have suspected.

Within two weeks we had an apartment on Central Park West and several good friends. The refrigerator was full. Jobs were offered to us. Life was beginning to look a lot better here than in the French Quarter, a place we had run away from when it stopped being hospitable to our illusions. My wife began to feel that she could have just about anything she wanted, eventually. But what she wanted most at that moment, and didn't have, was her period. We went to the nearest hospital. They demanded fifteen dollars for a pregnancy test. We talked them down to ten. The rabbit died.

We have been deeply devoted to and in love with our child ever since the moment we found out we were going to be parents. But my wife and I separated before our darling daughter was two, before she even had a respectable amount of hair on her head.

At the moment I write this, I am home from work because my daughter is sick. I have seized the silence of this day to report that, although six years ago I became a divorced single father with joint custody, I have never been happier or more contented in my life. Having never been a parent before, and not having a wife to turn to for help and support, a lot of the time I just plod through the darkness and hope I find my way to doing the right thing for my daughter. Yet sometimes I know intuitively what to do.

I am a very good father. I enjoy being a parent. I am very dedicated to my daughter. Celeste is eight now, and she is doing well.

The fact remains that my daughter is from a broken home. I think she would like me to be in a relationship with a woman for my sake, as well as for hers. But I'm in no hurry. Being a single parent isn't the best situation to be in. But it isn't necessarily the worst either. When you are home from work with a sick kid, it really doesn't matter if you're single or not. A sick kid who needs nurturing is a sick kid who needs nurturing, no matter what the specifics are.

This book is a glimpse into my relationship with my daughter. Because I am a writer, Celeste has been written about often. We have been on television together. I am not always happy that we have become an Exhibit A on how a parent and a child can triumph over difficult odds. My message is that you CAN overcome almost anything that you have been through. That doesn't mean you WILL. It also doesn't mean you will WANT to. But, if you wish to and if you try, you can turn your life around. Celeste and I are a success story. We are living proof that, if the sins of the father are visited on the son, then surely as well the blessings and health of the father can be visited upon the daughter.

I will be glad if our relationship can offer insight and hope to parents, as well as to adults who are considering having a child (or having BEEN a child). And to think that I was afraid to have a child for fear that I would not be able to parent well because I was not parented well! It isn't necessarily so. I should know.

Are Kids Beautiful?

"Aren't kids wonderful and beautiful?" I asked her.

"Of course they are!" she exclaimed as she was playing with her three-month-old granddaughter on her lap. "Nature makes them that way. Otherwise, who would put up with the crying and the dirty diapers—and having to stay home all the time? If it weren't for them being so cute and wonderful, it wouldn't be worth all the work. You'd just throw them away after you got bored or they stopped being fun."

What Do You Believe In?

Celeste was almost three. I was at my desk. She was staring out the window of her bedroom.

"Daddy?" she called to me.

"Yes?" I said absently, not looking up from my work.

"Do we believe in snow?"

I went into her room and looked out the window. The first snowfall that Celeste could remember had begun. It was snowing very hard. I looked at the joy-filled, silly look on her face. I kissed her on the forehead and we stared out the window together, in silence, for a long time.

I was struck by the immense power and responsibility I had in her life. Not only was she asking me to tell her what she believed in, she was also not making a clear distinction between herself and me. I was startled to realize just how huge a role I play in her life. I mean, of course I play a huge role in her life—I'm her father. But how could I ever have guessed just how important I am to her before a statement like that?

It's kind of scary. I'm afraid that I am going to make too many mistakes. I guess I will simply have to do the best I can. And I can see how this day will change my life. From now on, I will have to pay closer attention to the question Celeste prompted me to ask of myself: "Just what DO I believe in?"

There is one thing I am sure of:

I absolutely, positively, with all my heart, believe in children—and snow.

It's My Body

Celeste was four years old. Like any decent four-year-old, she was a mess every night. You know how four-year-olds are: they eat each other's food, spit in each other's hair, put unbelievable things into their pockets, fall off things that are impossible to fall off of, and balance on things that are impossible to balance on. And they come home real dirty.

"It's time for your bath, Celeste," I shouted to her as I ran the water in the bathtub.

"No."

"Celeste, you're dirty and stinky and you need a bath."

"No."

"Celeste, you're getting a bath whether you want one or not."

"It's MY body!!!"

I stared at her. Could I have heard her right? A four-year-old shouting feminist declarations at me? I guess she has already begun to learn about emotional and physical boundaries. Where did she learn this? Probably by listening to me. And her mother. Both of us have been working on these issues for a long time. It makes sense she would pick up on it. But at the age of four?

I try to imagine what happened to me as a four-year-old kid, when I witnessed all the violence in my house. No wonder it is such a struggle to change. And wow! What a blessing that my daughter is different and feels that she has a say in what happens to her, even at the ripe old age of four.

That is truly great! I am so proud of her!! But, I'll tell you what—she's still getting a bath.

The Nut with the Umbrella

I think Celeste was four at the time. I had picked her up from school and we were walking home when a sudden, summer rain struck. I had expected it. I'd brought along an umbrella. One umbrella. I was already carrying my satchel, and Celeste's backpack and lunch box, so I couldn't pick her up as well.

I held the umbrella over her head as we walked down the street. She was having a lot of fun. I was totally unprotected and completely drenched. There was no space anywhere on my body between my clothes and my skin. Wet. I looked into my satchel to see if it was too late to protect my writing. I saw a mass of blue, abstract ink drawings that used to be my words.

At the stoplight on Fifth Avenue, all the passengers in the cars stared at us through steamy windows. We must have been quite a sight. I rather liked the image, and that's why, despite my wretched drenchedness, I hadn't raced under a canopy to wait until the storm passed. I imagined the people in the cars were very impressed with what a loving father I was—offering all the protection to his daughter and none to himself. Yes. I'm that kind of guy.

We went to a restaurant. I sat down and felt a squish from my waterlogged pants. The air conditioning was on. We ate a soggy meal and left quickly. I got a bad cold the next day. I had to take Celeste to her mother's house because I was too sick to take care of her.

My reward for giving my all to my daughter had been nothing. Surrendering my needs to hers had not benefited me in any way—or her either. I was sick in bed. She was out in the park, playing with her mother. She had learned nothing from my sacrifice. I had done nothing to ensure that her future would be different from my past. Instead of being impressed with what a wonderful father I was, the people in those passing cars probably were wondering who the nut with the umbrella was.

Failing to protect myself, I had failed to protect my daughter.

Whose Homework Is This?

I was helping my five-year-old daughter with her homework.

"I feel like you are angry at me because I didn't get the answers right," she said to me.

I dropped my pencil and looked at her in stunned silence. I opened my mouth to lie to her, and then closed it without saying a word. She was right. I was upset because she wasn't getting the answers right, or quickly enough according to my timetable. I couldn't deny my feelings to her. She freaked me out when, at the ripe old age of five, she was able to detect, through my silence or attitude, what I was feeling.

This situation was no big deal in itself. But through it I discovered something important about my daughter and the course our relationship was going to take. I had taught her for every day of her life to determine, acknowledge, and accept all of her feelings. I had taught and demonstrated to her that she was free to talk about all of her feelings to me. And now that she was five—a very aware five, at that—she was beginning to take me up on my offer. I asked for it. I got it. A voice in my head told me that for the rest of my life, this child would feel free to hold me responsible for what I say to her and what I do.

I looked at my daughter, staring up at me from her homework. "I have been pushing myself very hard all day today," I said to her. "I came home and began to push you too. That isn't fair to you or to me. Sorry. Can we start your homework over again after dinner?"

"Sure," Celeste said.

And that is exactly what we did.

Intuition

I offered Celeste a choice of three desserts. She didn't want any of them. She wanted me to get dressed and go out and buy a dessert for her. I said no. She went into her room and cried for forty-five minutes.

Did I abandon her by not going into her room and comforting her? Would I be playing into a game of hers if I tried to rescue her? Did she need to get the crying out of her system? Was she in the other room floating in a sea of tears, unable to reach shore? Was this something she needed to work out by herself?

I hate situations like this, when I don't know how to be or what to do. I wished there had been someone there to help me. Perhaps the crying jag was something Celeste needed to work out, and my reaction to the crying was something I needed to work out.

Sometimes all you can do is sit and cry. You deserve noninterference from others, including a loving parent.

At times like these, I just grope around in my intuition and pray for guidance.

Milk Money

The teacher was killed in a car accident. All of her first-grade students were extremely hurt and confused by the event. Some of the children had learned about loss and separation through the death of a pet, but for many, this was their first experience with death. The death of this very significant person in their lives was their first exposure to loss, letting go, abandonment, and grief.

Members of the school staff, the school psychologist, and parents did an excellent job of helping the children deal with the feelings and issues of love, trust, fear, faith—all the swirling emotions that flow over the survivors of tragedy.

But there was one little girl who was not healing. She seemed to be a bit better by the end of the school day, but in the morning she would be right back in her state of despair. Every attempt was made to allow this little girl to grieve at her own rate. No one tried to hurry her along, even though the rest of the class was getting over it and the teacher had been replaced by an equally loving and responsible person.

The little girl, in fact, seemed to be getting worse. What began as moping around developed into depression. She had no energy to play. She had little concentration and was generally uncommunicative.

It was decided that intervention was necessary. Parents, teachers, and the school psychologist began to spend a lot of time talking to her about her teacher's death and what it meant to her. The child seemed to understand everything that was being said. She improved to the point that she appeared eager to move on, but was still unable to do so.

Finally, almost desperate, the parents asked the minister of the neighborhood church, which happened to be Unitarian-Universalist, to come and speak with their daughter. The minister spoke with her on three occasions. The purpose of the first meeting was just to get to know each other.

The second meeting convinced the minister that the child was holding a dark secret. The third meeting resulted in the problem being revealed.

Milk money.

At the time of the accident, the little girl owed her teacher milk money. She felt so terrible, so guilty. How would she ever be able to pay the teacher back now that she was dead?

Rather than immediately launch into a discussion on responsibility, guilt, forgiveness, and whatnot—the wise minister set up a meeting between the child and the husband of the deceased teacher. At that meeting, the little girl was able to give the few coins to the husband, as repayment for the borrowed milk money.

The little girl began to improve immediately. She was absolved of guilt by positive action, and she was proud of what she did. She had obtained closure with a person she had loved and lost. She had learned that the fear of loss need not outweigh the risk of loving. She had seen faith in action. She had experienced many people offering help. She had witnessed recovery by the survivors. She had learned that you need not withhold love in order to move on. She had learned to let go of grief. And she helped the husband of her former teacher as well.

But who would ever have guessed what was bothering the little girl? The child didn't know either, until many people had worked hard and long with her. A child—especially a young child—can find it really difficult to put words to feelings like guilt and sadness.

So much about good parenting is simply luck. Will you be able to happen across a solution like this before the problem corrodes the child's sense of self-worth? Maybe yes, maybe no. I believe a lot of what parenting is about, particularly with a first child, is just doing the best you can and having faith that your best will be good enough.

Asking for help is important too. I have one child. I have never been a parent before. Without asking for help, I remain in the dark. By exposing my feelings of inadequacy, I gain strength. And hope. And courage. And willingness to ask for help again.

Just One Wish

Celeste: Dad, if you had just one wish, what would you wish for?

Me: I would ask for God's will to be done. What would you wish for if you had just one wish?

Celeste: I would wish for a million more wishes.

X-Ray

A little boy fell out of a tree and broke his arm. His parents took him in the car to the hospital. The boy, surprisingly, was experiencing little pain. The parents told him he would have to have an x-ray taken of his arm.

"What's an x-ray?" the boy wanted to know, as he sat quietly between his parents in the front seat.

"An x-ray is when the doctor takes a picture of the bone to see if it is broken," his mother replied soothingly—reassuringly, she thought.

The boy began to panic! He screamed and cried and tried to crawl into the back seat. The mother wondered if perhaps the bone had shifted, causing him great pain. He was crying so hard he couldn't answer her questions. He cried all the way to the hospital, all the way through the admission procedures, all the way to the x-ray room. Despite the assurances of the very kind doctor and the comforting nurse and nurturing parents, he screamed his head off.

Finally, drastic measures had to be taken. They held the boy down and began to strap his arm to the x-ray table.

The boy stopped his screaming just long enough to say, "Don't let them peel my skin off!"

What? All those assembled looked at each other and then at the boy. Of course! That was it! How else could you take a picture of the bone unless you peeled the skin off?

Once the boy was told a little about how an x-ray works, he was fine. He lay still. The x-ray was taken. And the healing process began.

I believe that the only way to understand a child is to be able to think like one. The only way to be able to think like a child is to be able to reach back into your own childhood and, without judgment or criticism, allow yourself to feel your feelings the way you experienced them as a child.

Sometimes, just by virtue of growing up, an adult loses access to the magical vision of a child's world. Many adults think that part of the process of becoming an adult is to discard the experience of having been a child. I disagree. The most interesting adults I know are those who have retained the ability to see the world through childlike—not childish—eyes. That way you can couple the clear vision of a child with the wisdom of an adult. I practice keeping in touch with my inner child so I can better understand my daughter.

I also believe that the best way to find out what children are feeling is to watch them and to ask them. Don't wait for them to ask you. For instance, my daughter often doesn't know she is scared, or she is ashamed to admit it.

I watch her. And I ask her a few gentle questions. Sometimes she is blaming herself for something that is not her fault. Sometimes she is worried about her mother or a pet. Sometimes she doesn't want to tell me what is going on and that is okay.

Children get stuck. They apply their best logic, intelligence, and insight and still come up with the most bizarre answers and interpretations. Sometimes they harbor these feelings for years, undetected by loving parents, and they suffer needlessly.

My daughter has a right to not include me in what is going on inside her. But if she appears to need help, I can find out, without being meddlesome, how life looks from her perspective. She is quite often seeing the same thing as I am, but from a different angle.

I encourage her to get her feelings out. I let her goof up. I let her hide. I let her be angry and confused. I don't take her feelings, like fear and sadness, away from her because I can't deal with them. I let her learn to trust me with her scary secrets. I let her be a kid. Then she might not feel that having adults around is like having your skin peeled off. Then she might talk to me before the misinformation becomes part of her soul.

I cannot save my daughter, nor would I wish to save her, from all the craziness of life. Sometimes the craziness is the best part. But I can try to spare her some of the hauntings of unnecessary demons. I can do my best to talk to her when she is reacting inappropriately, or when her fear is disproportionate to the risk, or when her grief is disproportionate to the loss. Other than loving children, simply paying attention to them seems to be the most important part.

Strawberries

"It isn't fair!" Celeste shouted at me. That sentence had become her mantra and the banner under which she marched through childhood. She chanted it often, almost every day. It seemed to me that it was part of her apprenticeship to becoming a professional victim. She seemed to think that she was powerless over fairness. When the Scales of Justice would crash down on one side, she would collapse into a heap of apathy and inertia, and wait to be rescued from the smelly bog of unfairness. She would pout about fairness and then sit and wait for it to be bestowed upon her by some magical power, otherwise known as Daddy.

Fairness is a complex notion that baffles children, adults, business partners, and even entire nations. How could I convey to her that life is indeed not always fair, yet things seem to balance out, particularly if you take an active role in your life, instead of sitting and waiting for things to go your way? How could I explain to her that people are seldom concerned with fairness if they feel that their needs, desires, and dreams are met? How could I discuss with her why it is that the people who don't get enough are the ones concerned with fairness, and not the ones who get too much?

As I usually do, I decided to teach her this lesson by using a metaphor. Intellectual discussions never work as well as stories. I washed and trimmed a pint of deep red, fragrant strawberries. It was late February in New York City, hardly the fresh fruit season. But these strawberries were incredibly delicious, as if Mother Nature had conspired to help me teach my lesson.

As Celeste watched me preparing the berries, her tongue moved back and forth across her upper lip like a windshield wiper. I placed the strawberries in a pretty, white bowl and set it in front of her. They were gone in an instant. Houdini couldn't have made them disappear any faster. I don't think she was even breathing while she ate them.

With cheeks still stuffed to capacity, she looked up at me and said, "More."

"They're gone, Celeste. There aren't any more."

"Ahhh. That's not fair!" Celeste said, disappointed and making a sound like the air being let out of a bicycle tire.

This was my perfect opportunity to teach her about fairness. "How many strawberries did you have, Celeste?"

"I don't know."

"I only had one, which is okay. But do you think THAT is fair?" I asked.

"Who said you could have one?" she asked.

I stared at her. Now I was the one who wasn't breathing. The Zen master had just zinged me again. How could she possibly say something to me like that? I work so hard to impart wisdom and knowledge to her. Doesn't she realize that many people pay me to do this kind of work with them? Doesn't she know that in most cities you could put a down payment on an apartment for what it costs for a pint of strawberries in February in New York? Doesn't she know or care how hard I try? It isn't fair!

Oh, well. Just because I am ready to teach a lesson doesn't mean that my child is ready to receive it. My lesson was a flop. I got myself out of my victim state of mind, in which I felt I was suffering from parent abuse, by doing the next best thing to being understood that I could think of.

I went out and bought another pint of strawberries. I washed them and trimmed them and counted them out into two pretty, white bowls. One for you. One for me. One for you. One for me. Celeste watched me like a Swiss banker. There was an odd number of strawberries in the pint.

I thought this was a perfect opportunity to teach myself a lesson so, when Celeste wasn't looking, I popped it into my mouth.

Now I am wondering, was that fair?

Fight Fair

Celeste told me that she got in a fight with her friend. The other girl threw the first punch, so Celeste thought the fight was her friend's fault.

I asked Celeste what she had been saying or doing that might have made the girl want to hit her. Celeste thought that didn't matter. I thought it was time for a story.

I told my daughter that once upon a time I was at the restaurant where I worked when a fight broke out. The maitre d' had told the bartender to give him some drinks to give to the cooks. The bartender said that he didn't mind supplying drinks to the cooks, but it would have to be at the end of the shift, not at the beginning.

The maitre d' became very upset and said several naughty words to the bartender. Then he said, "Look, I am the maitre d' and you are only the bartender. Now give me the drinks!" The bartender jumped over the bar and the fight began.

Celeste looked ponderingly at me and then asked if there were any customers in the restaurant at the time of the fight. I told her that it was early in the evening and there were only two tables seated, but, yes, there were customers there.

Celeste asked me what I thought should be done. I told her that both people should be punished, perhaps given a week off without pay. I told her that violence is a terrible thing, and that people have the right to laws and rules to protect themselves from it. I also told her that both people usually contribute to a fist fight, no matter who threw the first punch.

I asked Celeste what she thought should be done. She paused a long time before she said, "Instead of making them not work for a week, I think the bartender should be the maitre d', and the maitre d' should be the bartender for a week."

Without any apparent resources other than her eight-year-old mind and spirit, Celeste had not only arrived at a way to make the people involved responsible for their actions, she also arranged it so that they wouldn't have to miss work, which would place a burden on their fellow workers, who would have to pick up the slack in their absence. In addition to that, she had apparently picked up on the more subtle aspect of my story, the pretense of superiority that one worker had over the other. All on her own, she had arrived at the wisdom of walking a mile in someone's shoes before you judge that person.

Out of the mouths of babes.

Picture Perfect

My wife, my one-year-old daughter, and I were standing at a beautiful location in Central Park. We had stopped to enjoy the view, and had no idea that it would be there where we would decide to end our marriage.

With that realization, we fell into a moment of pained silence. Suddenly some jerk wearing an ascot and a beret, with a cheap camera around his neck, appeared and said, "Oh, what a picture-perfect family! For only five dollars I will take a picture of you, and you will have it to cherish from this moment until forever!"

To which I replied, "Get out of here before I kill you!"

A look of utter confusion, followed quickly by terror, swept across his face as he made a rapid departure. My wife and I stared at each other. We looked down at our precious daughter, who was sleeping in her baby stroller. We gazed across Central Park Lake.

I wish I had purchased the picture. Imagine! A family portrait taken at the exact moment of divorce.

Unlimited Combinations

My daughter goes to a private school in Manhattan. One advantage of this private school is its small classroom sizes. There were eleven children in my daughter's second-grade class. Not bad for a city of eight million people.

Of the eleven children, eight are from broken homes. Of the eight, four had parents who remarried this year. Of the four, two had both parents remarry this year.

That means—and pardon any errors because I'm not particularly good at math—that there are eleven children in my daughter's second-grade class, with twenty-eight parents.

That also means that there are fifty-six grandparents. Unless, of course, some of those grandparents remarried. And you know they did. So let's be conservative and say there are about sixty grandparents for the eleven kids.

Can you imagine how silly we feel ordering folding chairs and cupcakes for the end-of-the-year school play and family picnic?

Parenting Myself and My Daughter

How can I be a decent single parent?

That was the question that confronted me when I staggered out of an unsuccessful marriage and found myself with joint custody of a two-year-old girl.

I had been brought up by parents who were not good for their children in many ways, not the least of which was their inability to be emotionally supportive of us. I was also the youngest child in my family and I had no experience with children. Presently, there was no wife, mother, or girl friend to turn to for help and advice. My task was to, somehow, learn to love and nurture my daughter the way I was never loved and nurtured.

I was brought up believing that the nurturing of a child was a woman's job. Now I had to assume both roles, that of being the nurturer (Mommy) and the discipliner (Daddy). I had to be the breadwinner at home as well as the grocery-buyer for the school fair. I sometimes had to give up my chair at management meetings in order to take a chair in the pediatrician's waiting room. I knew I had to become a Daddymommy without virtue of knowing what a good Daddy or a good Mommy is. There had been an absence of role models in my life to guide me. I was not encouraged by statistics that say poorly parented children grow up to be lousy parents.

I don't want to blame my parents for my problems. I am an adult and I want to take responsibility for my life. I don't want to get stuck in blame and anger. But part of accepting responsibility for myself is to determine who is accountable for what. All my life I had successfully avoided blaming my parents for anything because I simply couldn't handle looking at what had happened to me as a child. I certainly didn't pin all my problems on my parents. But I eventually took a searching and fearless look at where some of my behavior and character defects originated. I had to be willing to look at the things my parents had done right as well as the things they had done wrong, so as to get a balanced perspective of what went into the making of the person I am today. I tried to pin the tail on the donkey and say: this is what happened. This is what it felt like. This is how the way I was raised still plays itself out in my life today.

I discovered that a lot of my character defects are a result of the way I was parented. Holding my parents accountable allows me to see how a problem might have originated with them, but now it is I who perpetuates the problem by not taking responsibility for changing it.

A huge obstacle to holding my parents accountable for their parenting is my denial; I deny how difficult my childhood was. My most frequently used tool of denial is letting my parents off the hook. I let them off the hook even if it means I have to put myself on the hook in order to do it. I put myself on the hook by blaming myself the same way they always blamed me. I let them off the hook by finding some fault in myself that caused them to behave the way they did. I would tell myself, for example, that if only I had been a better son then they would have been better parents. As an adult I put myself on the hook by telling myself that I am merely an ungrateful blame-seeker, who won't let go of the past and continues to needle the two people who loved him the most.

Closer to the truth is that I have a desperate need to believe that those two people were better parents than they were. I don't want to face the fact that they were not there for me emotionally. I don't want to admit that my parents often acted in disregard of my well-being. I don't want to admit it because it hurts too much. I was treated with little respect by parents who had little respect for themselves. They had low self-esteem and they taught low self-esteem to their children. They couldn't love because they had never been loved. They simply didn't know how to do it.

And, lo and behold, I found myself in the same situation with my daughter as my parents found themselves in with me. I had to act as if I knew what the hell I was doing in raising my daughter. I joined an organization of single parents and began to ask for help. I joined another organization that deals with the problems of adults who were raised in dysfunctional homes. There I learned that the feelings of pain, loss, perpetual disappointment, and fear of intimacy do not simply go away. They had remained lodged in me like a fish bone caught in my throat. I had to allow myself to feel those painful feelings that I had tried so hard to avoid all my adult life. I had to learn to talk about them with understanding people.

I learned that becoming a better parent would begin by parenting myself in the way that I was never parented. I had to acknowledge the existence of the child within me, the little boy inside the man, and I had to give that child all the love and respect he deserved but never got. The beginning of being good to my daughter was also the beginning of being good to myself. It is no small job.

My daughter is very different from the way her father was as a child. She is warm and outgoing, calm, willing to take risks, secure in the knowledge that she will not be punished for mistakes. She knows she has rights. She is proud of her work. She feels she is an important person whose contributions are appreciated. She has a basic belief in the fundamental goodness of people. She is not naive. She knows that evil and danger exist, but that is not the focal point of her universe. The moment my daughter was born and opened her eyes, I was the first person she saw. The first words I said to her were, "You are a child of God and you have been placed in my care. You do not belong to me and never shall. Welcome to your life. I am here to love you forever."

Living up to my commitment to my daughter has led me to a new and better way of loving other people and myself. My dual role of Daddymommy has allowed me to embrace the feminine as well as the masculine sides of myself. Consequently, I feel I am a more whole person than I was in my marriage. Then I leaned on a woman to provide the care for our child, which I felt incapable of simply because I am a man. I am a single, male parent, yet I have achieved a marriage of love and logic, of empathy and discipline. I lift weights at my health club and then go shopping for my daughter's panties and stockings. I supervise a staff of fifty men during the day, and cook meals and care for my daughter at night. I have discovered that I am more flexible than I ever suspected. And more loving.

    I can see now that because of my painful past, I have gained strength that my parents never had. So in a strange way, I find I am not only grateful that I survived my childhood, but I am grateful FOR my childhood. Without my wounded youth, I might have become more complacent, less intensely involved with and appreciative of the miracle of raising a child. Being a part of my daughter's life has helped me to become reconciled to my past, grateful for the present, and hopeful about the future.

Act as If

I am convinced it takes three to make a family, and my daughter and I are two, so what are we to do? Besides, there is no precedent for getting better in my family. We only know how to get worse. If I were talking about sickness, instead of health, I would have all the answers.

But my daughter is doing well, and there is more to it than pure luck. My parents claim they raised me, although the truth is that I raised myself, growing like a dandelion at the edge of a road. They appeared to not love themselves. They didn't act as if they loved each other. They certainly didn't know how to love me. How could I possibly know how to parent?

I have learned to ask for help, even though it goes against every cell in my body. Asking for help breaks the code of silence that governed my life until very recently. The message from my parents was that they would punish me, either physically or with silence, if I dared tell anyone what was going on within our home. I tried to keep my mouth shut. I tried to figure out the answers all by myself. But the pain became too great for me to bear.

Now, I ask for help. I have been so frightened that I would mess up my daughter's life. But every indication is that I must be doing something right. Celeste appears to be a break in the chain of addiction, violence, and craziness that has wrapped itself around my family for generations.

What I am finding so difficult to say is that I need help in raising my daughter. And just by saying that I need help opens up a previously cluttered space in me. It is a space where new ways of dealing with old problems can grow. Answers come to me now because I am ready to receive them.

I need help. I am not ashamed to admit it. I am not afraid to say it. I need help.

Help!

Doing It Backwards Is Right

I was doing some exercises on the living room floor. Celeste, aged five, was sitting on the couch, drawing. "I made a book," she said, "and I am going to put the telephone numbers of all my friends in it. Go get your address book and read the numbers to me and I will copy them into my book." When she was finished she proudly handed the book to me. One of the phone numbers I saw looked like this:

558-7819 (written with some digits reversed)

I complimented her on her work and said to her, "I have to tell you that two of the numbers are backwards."

"They are not," she said.

"I must be honest with you and tell you that they are."

"I have the right to write them the way I want to."

"Yes you do. And I have the right to tell you that they are backwards." She became extremely frustrated and put the book away.

Later that morning I told her teacher what had happened and how I had corrected her, and he said, "Don't do it. By writing the numbers she is working a little beyond her ability as it is. One day she will look at the page and say to herself 'this number is backward' and she will correct it. The potential harm lies in her deciding not to do the work because it doesn't please you."

What Celeste had wanted by showing the book to me was validation for her efforts. She wanted to be appreciated and encouraged for trying to reach a little beyond her ability to learn something new. Her self-respect and her confidence were the real issues here, much more so than learning how to master the writing of numbers.

My reaction to learning this was interesting: it made me sick to my stomach. I felt as if I had damaged her terribly by trying to correct her. Gradually, I gained a healthier perspective of the situation. I congratulated myself on perceiving the possible error so quickly. The problem came up, and one hour later I had already discussed it with her teacher. Yet the throb in my stomach persisted. I allowed myself a couple of hours to get into the feeling.

As a child I was always being corrected. The object of the correction was to make me as much like my parents as possible. Yet they were sick people, and their beliefs and behavior and attitudes vacillated tremendously from day to day, sometimes hour to hour. I was trained to spell something the way they spelled it, whether that was the way it appeared in the dictionary or not. There was no time to relax and be myself. There was no time to experiment with different ways of doing things. There was one way to put on a shirt, to answer a phone, to speak to my mother, to do the dishes, to say goodnight. There was one way to think, and that was to think just like Dad. Anything else was treason. I became very rigid in my thinking. Experimentation was heresy. Dogma was divine. Mistakes were openly ridiculed.

Now I am an adult and I am saying that it is fine that my daughter writes her numbers backwards.

Life is weird. This task of dismantling my life is amazing. I am writing my life backwards. I am trying to be open and flexible, to realize that my daughter knows more about being a child than I do. In a strange way I am asking her to help me be her parent. And she is. I don't need all this control. My daughter and I are growing up together. It isn't as difficult as I thought it would be.

Transition

There are certain milestones that mark the growth of every child. Just yesterday my six-year-old and I were sitting on a bus on the way home from school, discussing the difference between a five- and a six-point star. We were adorable. I could tell by the look on the faces of several people who were watching us.

Suddenly my daughter did something that ranks right up there with the other milestones of her life, such as her first step, her first solid food, and her first spoken word. My darling six-year-old turned to me and gave me the finger. Such progress! Such growth! Such independence! Such a New Yorker! Such a good time I had watching the faces of the people change who were watching us. Fourteen mouths fell open all at once.

We adults had collectively witnessed the collapse of the age of innocence in a young girl's life. I told Celeste that it was an inappropriate gesture. "Inappropriate" is the modern-day equivalent of the word I was raised with, which was "naughty."

I rang the bell and we ended our ten-minute bus ride somehow much older. This was a milestone I was not quite prepared for. Celeste was suddenly more worldly. She had a bold look in her eye. Her cheeks were flushed with a sense of accomplishment. She had registered a strong reaction in the adults around her, and I could tell it felt good to her, even though she didn't know exactly how she had done it. She seemed to have enjoyed the look of shock that swept my face when she gave me the finger.

Celeste is a true member of the world now. She no longer exists only under my wing. A lot of what she says and does and learns is out of my control. There was no thought of punishment. She didn't know what it meant. She knew it was "a curse." But she was just showing me something new she learned at school. I told her not to do it again, and she agreed.

A daddy and his baby got on the bus, and a father and his daughter got off.

All That Is Left

I was having dinner in a restaurant with my daughter, who is halfway through the second grade.

"How are you doing, kiddo? How are things at school?"

"I don't know," she said. "You see, when I do something really good, the teacher gets all excited and claps her hands and smiles. But I don't get excited about it at all."

Oh, no! It's hereditary! She's just like her old man!

How could my daughter feel that way? She does well in private school. She does well in just about everything. She has two loving parents. I write books and articles on my relationship with her. I dedicate the better part of my life to her. And yet here she is, at the ripe old age of seven, finding herself unable to accept the good things that are being said about her.

Celeste's life and experience is contrary to her father's, yet we are so much alike. I once went to an astrologer because the visit was given to me as a birthday present. I didn't even tell the astrologer that I had a daughter, but she said to me: "Don't worry if your daughter is a little bossy. Don't be alarmed about the things she says. It might seem that she is strangely mature for her age. That is because she used to be your mother in a former life."

That message was intended to comfort me!

Oh, boy! Once again I am pitted against my powerlessness over the ultimate course of Celeste's life, as well as my own. The best I can do is all I can do.

The Last Day of School

It was the end-of-the-year party for the second grade. Everyone had brought a dish of food or something to drink. The children were posing for pictures with the teacher and their schoolmates. The parents were reminiscing. Desks were being cleaned out and each item was explained at length. It was a lovely occasion.

I had to go to the bathroom. It was down the hall from the classroom. As I left the classroom and entered the hall, I was stampeded by about a dozen children. They were shouting and running, slipping on puddles of soda. One child took whole, green grapes into his mouth and blew them like cannonballs at his friends. It was a sure sign of affection! One kid grabbed me by either side of my shirt and moved me around like a floor lamp he was hiding behind so he wouldn't get hit by the flying grapes. How intimate, considering we didn't know each other. Three boys were leaning their shoulders against the door to the girls' bathroom, trying to get in. Each time the door would open a little, there would be a peal of screams by the girls who, with equal force, were trying from the other side to keep the door closed. These children were first-graders.

When I returned to my daughter's classroom, it seemed so genteel. It was like a cocktail party. My daughter was in second grade. The kids in the halls were only one year younger. Wow! What a difference! I'm not sure I like it.

What happened to my grubby little kid? What will be next? We can't hold hands? This all happens so fast. These monstrous sneakers are lying around our apartment. If they weren't pink with drawings on them, I would think they were mine.

And what about me? I look in the mirror much more often since that party. Is there a time in my life when one single year will mark the turn from young adult to "looks pretty good for his age"? I have seen it happen to other people. I return to the place where I take my summer vacation and the young woman I had a crush on now looks like an early middle-aged executive. Scary. I cling precariously to all definitions of youth. And I realize that the greatest yardstick of an adult's age is watching the growth of a child.

Am I beginning to look silly in this sleeveless tee shirt with Boris and Natasha from the Bullwinkle Show on it? Does anyone even remember the Bullwinkle Show? Should I take it off? Well? What do you think?

I Want What I Want When I Want It

She was cranky when I picked her up at school. For a brief moment, there was joy at seeing Daddy. But it was quickly followed by the baited question, "What are we going to do tonight?"

I have heard that question enough to know what it really means. It means that my daughter knows exactly what she wants to do and if I don't want to do the same thing, or at least let her talk me into it, then there will be a price to pay.

"First we have to pick up our laundry," I began.

"Ohhh!" Celeste sounded like she had just been stabbed.

"Then we are going home to have pasta and salad for dinner. I have some fresh basil leaves which I am going to crush in a bowl of olive oil and . . ."

"I don't want to pick up the laundry! I want to go to the hamburger restaurant. Please!" She was enjoying the echo of her newly seven-year-old voice as it resonated in the stairwell of her school.

The next thing I knew I was staring at the laminated menu in the hamburger restaurant, which has all the charm of a hospital cafeteria.

It bothers me to be led around New York City with a ring through my nose by a seven-year-old. But I was seriously torn. I could feel this immense neediness in her. She was clingy and tired, and there was an aura of sadness about her. I could sense her emotions swirling around inside of her, but very little was coming out. I was concerned and confused. She didn't know what was going on inside of her any more than I did. It was useless to talk pop psychology to a seven-year-old. I was trying to act like she wasn't driving me crazy, which was probably driving HER crazy.

She became progressively bossier and pushier as the evening dragged on. The hamburger restaurant, as I had tried to explain to her, had not been the solution she was looking for.

When we got home I raised my voice at her, which is something I rarely do. The tropical rainforests in her eyes hit the monsoon season. She cried and yelled and snorted and thrashed and basically fell apart.

My initial impression was that she was finally getting what she had wanted all along: ventilation. She had unleashed the anger, sadness, and frustration that was pent up inside of her. I viewed it as the spiritual equivalent of vomiting. I remain convinced today that a lot of my own problems are rooted in having stuffed my feelings way down inside of me, out of reach, swallowed whole, never fully digested. As a kid I had always refused to purge my hidden feelings for fear of getting punished. So I was glad Celeste felt safe enough to get her feelings out with me.

But somehow, somewhere, a boundary was crossed. I began to feel that I was being verbally abused by my own daughter. I didn't want to censor her, or to disallow her access to her feelings because I wasn't in the mood to hear about them. But I also didn't want to get thrashed by this little runt who thinks her father is a pushover. We had a conversation and I disagreed with what she was saying.

"Now wait a minute! I was talking!" she said, while pointing her forefinger at me.

"You were not talking," I informed her calmly. "You were shouting. Do you think you can tell me what you want to tell me without shouting?"

"No!" she shouted.

I warned her that her behavior was destined to result in me punishing her.

"Well, why didn't you tell me that in the beginning of our fight," she asked, "instead of waiting until the very end and then shouting at me? Why didn't you say it nice a long time ago?"

Little kids are often way too smart for me. They ask great questions. But how do you explain that when someone starts out being nasty to you, you try to ignore it because that seems so much easier than confronting the situation head on? How do you tell a child about giving someone the "benefit of the doubt"? How do you explain to a child the difference between being verbally abusive and standing up for your rights? How do I tell Celeste that, because I am a single parent, there is no partner to turn to to ask how I am doing, or if I am being too strict. How do I compensate for the fact that, because my child lives with me only half the week, I have no way of knowing what happened at her mother's house the night before that might have precipitated such an explosion of feelings?

Moments later, the monsoon rains in my child's eyes had subsided as quickly as they had arrived and we were sitting on her bedroom floor trying to assemble a new dresser. We were listening to her favorite record and she was petting her hamster when she looked up at me and said, "We're good again."

"Being good has nothing to do with getting angry, Celeste. You can argue and still be good. You can even do something wrong and still be good. And no matter what happens, no matter what we're like, I will always love you. You know that already, though, don't you, Celeste?"

She nodded her head as if there wasn't the slightest doubt, which is the way it has been between us since the day she was born. All the manic behavior, the nastiness, the sadness and pain, had been rinsed away. She was calm and ready to go to sleep. I put her to bed, and rubbed her back until her breathing grew shallow and her face relaxed.

Was I a pushover? Was I appropriate? Was I wrong to let her shout at me, or was it good to let her get her feelings out? Should I react the same way if she does it again? If she is too young to tell me, how can I possibly find out what is inside her that is hurting her so much?

I went into my room and placed my hands on either side of a full-length mirror and leaned my face close to my reflection. After staring in the mirror at this, my only companion, I wondered if I will ever know what the hell I am doing.

Are My Feelings Okay with You?

Celeste is on the phone with her friend:
Hello, Sue! I just called to ask you to pay attention to me at your birthday party tomorrow.
(Long pause.)
Well, yeah, I want you to pay attention to ALL the children and to me too.
(Long pause.)
Well, I really called to ask you to pay attention to everybody.
Yeah. Yeah. I know.
(Long pause.)
Well, you can pay attention to anybody you want and it really doesn't matter if it's me or not.
(Long pause.)
Well, it's okay. Doesn't matter. I don't care. Yeah. Okay. Sure. Good-bye.
(Click.)
Celeste didn't know what hit her. She walked dejectedly into the other room and turned her attention to something else. But I knew what hit me: seeing how people eventually can become reluctant about being totally honest with someone. I heard only one side of my daughter's phone conversation. But I could see and hear Celeste becoming embarrassed about her insecurity and her desire for love, attention, and acceptance. I could sense the beginning of her feeling that there is something wrong with having needs, that she had no right to ask for or expect a little extra when she was feeling especially needy. She began to talk herself out of her feelings because of the other person's response to them. I saw her learning how to hide her true self and how to define herself according to what other people want her to be.

Is this called socialization? Is this inevitable? Is this becoming realistic and learning to compromise? Is this growing up? Is it my job to help her to become reconciled to not always getting what she feels she needs, or should I teach her to learn early in life not to let people talk her out of her feelings?

Even though a certain response is socially sanctioned ("you gotta learn to toughen up," "you can't always get what you want," "sticks and stones can break my bones," "nice guys come in last"), that doesn't mean it will work.

No matter what anybody says, there is no right or wrong answer to these questions.

Birds and Bees

Celeste, her best friend, Tyler, and I were sitting in a coffee shop. Tyler said that her mother and father were thinking about having another baby. We talked for a few more moments until Celeste said, "Hey, wait a minute! You say your mom is thinking about having another baby. I don't understand. What does THINKING have to do with having a baby? I mean, how do you THINK a baby into your belly?"

Tyler laughed and laughed and said to me, pointing to Celeste. "She doesn't know!"

Celeste turned to me, looking dejected and laughed-at, and said, "Doesn't know what?"

Oh, my God! I said to myself, I knew this day was coming. But I am not prepared to talk to my daughter about the birds and the bees for the first time in a crowded coffee shop with her worldly young friend egging me on. I looked at the faces of the two beautiful children waiting for me, the pillar of wisdom and adulthood, to answer them.

"Ask your mother about that when you see her tomorrow," I finally said.

Wow! I chickened out! I didn't think I would, but I did. Part of me believes that since mine is an opposite-sex child, her mother should tell her. And another part of me knows that I would wimp out of this situation, no matter what.

Celeste has since talked to her mother about it. I asked, and Celeste told me she doesn't have any questions about sex. I certainly do, but that's another story. Right now I'm mostly dealing with the fact that my baby, the subject of so much of my writing, my tiny connection to innocence, is now an eight-year-old third-grade New Yorker who knows about sex.

Wow! This growing up happens fast! You don't get much time to think about what you're doing. But then again, what does THINKING have to do with it?

Dinosaur Diarrhea

Celeste was studying dinosaurs in her school science program. She was telling me about her latest discoveries when a distant look swept across her face.

"Just why did the dinosaurs become prestinked?" she wanted to know.

"Extinct," I said.

"Yeah."

"Well," I said sagely, stroking the wisdom beard that I never bothered to grow, but which mystically appears whenever the correct question is asked of me. "The latest theory—that means an idea you arrive at from looking at a lot of facts—is that they became extinct because of diarrhea."

Celeste looked at me as if I were cracking another one of my borderline jokes, the kind that bypass the solid ground of conventional humor in order to teeter on the edge of absurdity and perversity.

"It's true," I continued. "I mean, I'm not positive that is what happened. I wasn't there. But I really did read that in a fancy magazine for grown-ups."

Celeste stared at me for a moment and then changed the subject.

Yesterday I got Celeste's school report from the first semester of the third grade. Her science teacher wrote that the class was learning Newton's Law of Motion and studying laws of gravity, inertia, friction, and many other things. She also wrote, "What a delightful child and student Celeste is! She is curious, determined, and steadfast in all of her endeavors. She works hard on all of her experiments and she records data and results in her own personal scientific folder. She shares easily her wealth of background material, and is willing to 'give up' her misconceptions (that dinosaurs only died of diarrhea). She is cooperative and displays greater tolerance for the opinions of others. I have enjoyed her in class!"

I had a tremendous laugh about that note from her teacher. I can just imagine Celeste proudly telling all her classmates about dinosaur diarrhea. I was also struck by how good Celeste's memory is. But, most of all, I was almost overwhelmed by the power that even the slightest things I say have over Celeste.

Being a parent is a tremendously powerful position to be in. It scares me sometimes. We parents tread a delicate line between being cautious in what we say (so as not to prejudice or misinform) and being TOO careful (so that we lack spontaneity and originality).

I guess that because I grew up feeling not listened to, it is hard for me to believe that I am being listened to now. A lot of my writing, publishing, and public speaking is part of a continuing attempt—finally—to be heard. I want my truth to be heard, and I don't mind my mistakes being heard either. I think it is good that Celeste can accept someone's words— even her own father's—as just another opinion. I have the right to be wrong.

When Celeste comes home from school today, we will talk about opinions, facts, and laws. Then I will introduce her to a new word: theory. I want Celeste to learn that she doesn't have to choose between her teacher's opinion and her father's. She has the right to arrive at her own conclusion, even if the conclusion is that she doesn't know or care.

After years of tending a very young child, I find it rewarding that Celeste is now old enough so that we can have a conversation, and she can hold up her end of it very well. Tonight we will have a lovely dinnertime conversation about dinosaur diarrhea.

Asthma Attack!

The school nurse told me that Celeste had an allergy attack earlier that day. She had such a hard time breathing, she couldn't assemble her inhaler. The teacher had never seen an inhaler before, and couldn't assemble it either.

"Why didn't you tell us that Celeste uses an inhaler?" the nurse wanted to know. "Why didn't you tell us that Celeste has asthma? Why didn't you show us how to assemble the inhaler? Why didn't you leave one here in the nurses' station in case of an emergency like this?"

Because I'm a despicable person, I thought to myself, but what I actually said was, "You're right. I should have. I didn't know. I have never been the parent of a seven-year-old girl before, and I don't always get it right. I'm sorry. Now I know. Besides, the allergist never indicated that the asthma was this severe. He never implied that this might happen. He must have underestimated the severity of her case. She might be getting worse. I have to go back to him and find out. In the meantime, I will get a prescription for another inhaler and keep it, already assembled, in the nurses' station."

The above mentioned event happened a month ago. I am still trying to get over it. In the middle of my forehead I have a flashing, red SHAME button with a sign above it that says PUSH ME. Everyone I know can see the button, and many people push it liberally. I push it a lot myself.

I'm glad that I didn't use my daughter's asthma attack as an opportunity to punish myself. I must constantly remind myself that I am not a "bad" person trying to become a "good" person. I am a troubled person trying to get better. I make mistakes, but I am not a mistake. I am a perfectly imperfect parent. If I tell my daughter it is okay to make mistakes, learn from them, and move on—then it is about time I allow myself the same love and acceptance. If I punish myself for doing something wrong, then I will begin to refuse—stubbornly—to admit I was wrong, in order to avoid self-punishment.

    Celeste's asthma, by the way, became a lot better after her mother's marriage took place. Celeste is fine now. I am fine. It's time to let go of this one.

This Is a Test

"What is my babysitter's name?"

"You ask me that all the time, Celeste. I can't believe that you don't remember. Her name is Kathy."

"You're right," Celeste said to me.

"What do you mean, I'm right? You act surprised that I know. It seems that you are testing me."

"I am," she said.

"Why?"

"To see if you're my real dad."

"What do you mean by THAT?"

"I just want to make sure that someone didn't switch you with someone who looks and talks like you, but isn't you. I don't want a different you to put me to bed. I want to make sure that you are you. So I make up these tests."

"Did I pass the test tonight?"

"Yeah. Good night, Daddy. I love you."

"I love you too."

I kissed her goodnight, turned out the light, and left the room. I sat at the kitchen table and asked myself what my mother's name was. I answered correctly. Then I asked myself, What was the name of my second grade teacher who had a dream that I would become president of the United States? I answered that one correctly also.

Now both my daughter and I are convinced that I am myself.

Maybe she was on to something. Sometimes I don't know who I am. I have changed so much in the past couple of years, I hardly recognize myself. Perhaps she notices those changes and is confused by them. When she was very little I must have appeared ageless and timeless and as boundless as the sky. Perhaps now that she is getting older, she is learning that I am actually more like a vapor rising off a puddle of gasoline. I am like the ribbon of squiggly lines above the hot, black asphalt of a desert highway. Perhaps she has noticed that if she looks closely, she can see right through me. Perhaps she senses that I won't always be here.

When she glances through our photo album and sees me looking very different at thirty-eight than I looked at twenty-eight and even more different than I looked at eighteen, perhaps she thinks of my life not as a continuum during which I gradually age, but looks at each photo as if it's of an entirely different person. Could the young boy with the angelic face and the long hair possibly be her daddy? How could he possibly have changed into this man with the wisdom lines around his eyes?

I think her suspicions are correct. I am a different person today than I was yesterday, than I will be tomorrow. I am created anew each day. So much of my pain is related to trying to drag a former self into the body I inhabit today. With a bus ticket good for only yesterday, I wander around the depot of myself looking for a connection. I try to move back into the haunted houses of my past and don't understand why the sheets smell moldy.

My daughter's father is many people. She is right to devise a test to see who I am today. Sometimes I don't recognize me either because I grow and change so quickly that I can't keep up with the changes. Life is a process of unveiling the many layers of myself, or should I say "myselves." My closets contain the clothes of a hundred people. And I must make room for the hundred people in me yet to be born.

Once again I have learned something important from my daughter. I think I will wait a few years to tell her about this. Or does she already know?

Kids and Money

In preparation for the laundry, I searched through Celeste's pockets and found four one-dollar bills.

"Wow! Look what I found! And it was in your pockets, so that means it's your money!" I handed the money to Celeste who, without a word, put the bills on the kitchen counter and walked away.

It was then that I realized she had no respect for or understanding of money. I made her that way. My parents were constantly worried about money. The worrying never produced one additional cent, but it did produce a lot of anxiety. I made a decision at the time of the first visit from the Tooth Fairy (who was a philanthropist, as it turned out) that Celeste should be spared anxiety about money. Money was simply not that important.

A couple of years later Celeste and I took a little girl on a play date with us. We ended up in a gift shop looking for "just one little thing." The little girl had twenty-five cents with her. Celeste had $6.00. In the interest of fairness, Celeste gave $3.00 to the little girl. That means the little girl had $3.25 and Celeste had $3.00. Neither of them had any problem with that. I tried to dissuade Celeste from giving away half of her money. She didn't have any problem with it. She simply wasn't uptight about money. That meant that she didn't have any respect for money either. I wonder where she got that?

Celeste has also never received an allowance. She is not a greedy child. She is very reasonable, and accepts my saying that I would like to buy her current interest—whatever it may be—for her, but I don't have the money. Celeste is not extravagant. I have enough money to buy her what she needs. An allowance seemed utterly unnecessary.

But my nonchalance about money is beginning to catch up with us. I realized that I have the same attitude about money as Celeste does. I bounce a check occasionally, not because I don't have the money. (I do.) I don't bounce a check because I resent paying bills either. (I don't.) I bounce checks because I forget about and lose paychecks.

It is not good for Celeste to grow up underestimating and not respecting powerful tools, like money. Perhaps we can strike a balance between denial and obsession. I am going to include Celeste in the financial aspect of our household. And I am going to grant both of us an allowance. Then perhaps money will take its rightful place in our lives.

Just Say Yes

I was raised on "no," so now I try to say yes to almost everything, unless I have a very good reason not to. So when my former wife asked me if my daughter, Celeste, could go to Cape Cod to visit her grandparents, I said, "Yes."

"It will be for six weeks."

I paused and said, "Yes."

A couple of days passed and I got another call from my former wife. "Can Celeste go with me to Greece?"

I paused again and said, "Yes."

"But it will be for three more weeks. Is that okay?"

"Yes."

"We will be leaving directly from the Cape. We won't be back in New York as originally planned. Is that okay?"

"Yes."

An hour or so after I hung up, I realized that Celeste would be gone for nine consecutive weeks. Two things struck me. One was that I would be able to knock around New York that summer without having to worry about being a parent. I would be able to write every morning and stay out late every night. The second thing was my concern about whether Celeste could handle that amount of time without me.

I know now that I was the one who could not handle that amount of time without HER. A small part of me thinks that any pain at all is bad, and should be avoided at all costs. In the midst of my deepest pain of missing Celeste, I was crying and trying to tie my shoelace, which I couldn't do because I couldn't see through the tears. I said out loud to myself, This is hell! I don't want to live like this anymore. There is too much pain in this life. Just how much am I supposed to be able to take?

Then I heard another voice, not as loud but just as strong, inside my head saying, This is life! What are you trying to escape? What you are trying to avoid is not hell, it is life!

I felt that I had volunteered for something I was not prepared to handle.

I called my former wife and insisted that Celeste be allowed to come and visit me for the weekend before she went to Greece. When the weekend came, I had made virtually no plans. I had forgotten, or perhaps I never realized, how it often doesn't really matter what Celeste and I plan to do. We always manage to have a good time. Just being together is what counts.

I picked up Celeste at the airport. She had flown alone. Her grandparents had put her on the plane and a stewardess had taken care of her during the flight. Celeste is a peaceful, loving, trusting child. As I watched Celeste and the stewardess walking toward me down the corridor that leads from the plane to the terminal, I could see how much fun they were having together. I thought about my own childhood. I too would have been very excited about flying without a grown-up. But I also would have been very frightened that no one would be there to pick me up when I reached my destination. I would have asked myself questions like, Did my parents remember how to get to the airport? Did they sleep through the alarm? Are they drunk? Are they in the airport bar?

And yet, there was my daughter walking confidently toward me. I don't think she is capable of such thoughts as I would have had. The thought of me not being there to pick her up would be as absurd to her as putting vinegar on ice cream.

Celeste and I had a great Saturday together. The next morning she set three places at the table. I asked who the third one was for. "It's for God," Celeste said matter-of-factly. I didn't question it then, and I don't question it now. Perhaps she knows something I don't. I have always felt that children are in perfect touch with a spiritual world, until we adults begin to talk them out of it.

We went to the newly renovated Central Park Zoo. We went back to the Carousel. We had a picnic lunch behind the American Museum of Natural History. We took a long walk and went to another playground.

We were having a wonderful time until, suddenly, a sense of hollowness, longing, grief, purposelessness, fear, and sadness overtook me. All these pathetically familiar feelings, which I had known so many times in my childhood, were back. In fifteen minutes I had to turn Celeste over to her mother and would not see her again for nine weeks. It would be autumn when she returned. Part of me wanted to return her to her mother right away, and get the inevitable pain of separation over with. Another part of me wanted to stretch the fifteen minutes into three years, the way only a child knows how to do.

I did not want to let go. Celeste didn't want to go either. She sat in my lap. It was a hot day, and we were both sweating, but Celeste wanted to stay close to me. I wanted to divert her attention, to break away from this intense waiting for the moment of separation to occur. I offered her an ice cream or soda if we would only walk to the nearby store to get it. She would have no part of my plot. She wanted what she already had—love.

I was slipping back into my old stance of love not being worth the pain and the risk. She too was sad about us parting, but she did not feel the need to pull back in the futile attempt to protect herself. The sadness made her closer to me, not farther away.

Despite my claims to the contrary, my fear of intimacy does extend to my daughter. My feelings now about Celeste were the same as the feelings I had when her mother and I separated. I felt at that time that I should withhold love from my daughter in order to protect myself from the inevitable pain of separation. I feared her mother would get custody. (She didn't. We were awarded joint custody.) I feared her mother would leave town with her (She didn't, and was prohibited from doing so by the divorce stipulation even if she wanted to, which she didn't.)

I saw how my fear was irrational, especially since I had taken concrete emotional and legal steps to protect myself. I saw how fear can incapacitate me and drive me mad with incessant worrying. I also saw how fear can cause me to become unable to take the risks necessary to get to where I want to be.

My running away from pain or conflict didn't begin with my marriage or the birth of my child. I have always been a leading practitioner of escape. When I was eighteen years old, someone published a poem about me. One of the lines in it was "Hurt me and I'll run away." He saw it. I didn't. But I see it now. When it comes to fight or flight, I'm gone!

The problem with running away is: I don't get to deal with many intimacy issues. I know a lot about courtship, but very little about staying put when things get difficult. When the going gets tough, I get going right out the door. If leaving was hard, as when I was married, I simply withdrew into my head and refused to come out. I did all that in exchange for the illusion of safety by trying to reconcile the way I did things in the past with the way I wished to do things differently now.

Now I had created a tricky problem for me. In order to truly love Celeste, I felt I had to let go of her. But I didn't want to confuse letting go with the withholding of love. How could I still love her and yet not be crippled by the fear of losing her? I wanted to let go of fear, but I wasn't willing to be one of those men who stop loving their children after the divorce because the children remind them so much of their former wife.

It was three o'clock, the appointed hour. I walked Celeste to her mother's house. Celeste clung to me at the door. Her mother invited me in, something I could tell she didn't want to do, but which she was doing to ease the separation problem for Celeste. I drank some juice out of my former glass as I stood in my former living room and watched my former wife pack my former suitcase for a summer vacation in Greece with her fiance and my daughter. "They look like such a nice family," I said to myself as panic invaded every cell of my body and blood raced to my legs in preparation of my usual flight from the scene of the hurt. Beads of sweat that felt like little balls of Crisco began to appear on my shoulders. A child's voice was screaming so loudly inside of me I almost told it to shut up. It was saying, "Don't leave me! Don't leave me!" I ignored the voice of the child within me, temporarily.

Sometimes it is appropriate to be an adult, no matter how childlike you're feeling.

    I silently sipped my juice. I watched them pack until I couldn't stand it any longer. I was there long enough for Celeste to see that their leaving was okay with me. That would help her to relax and have a good time without feeling that she was betraying me. I said something reassuring to Celeste. I don't remember what. We kissed and hugged goodbye. I could feel in our hug that the bond between us was alive and intact. I felt calmer. I felt a trip to Greece, even a trip to death, could not break our bond. Celeste was in good hands. Her mother and future stepfather would take good care of her.

    I bicycled through Central Park, crying behind my sunglasses. The breeze dried my tears before they fell below the rims of my glasses. No one could see me crying. Numbness began to move in like a marsh fog at twilight. My heart slowed. My breathing became shallow. I felt sleepy.

    I went home. The first thing I noticed were Celeste's little, red shoes sitting beneath the kitchen table. Everything was so still. My home felt like a place where I used to live. I went into Celeste's room and saw the mess that I had forgotten to ask her to clean up. Boy, was that a mistake! Her crayons, paper, unfinished drawings, hamster food, pajamas, and books were just where she had left them that morning. So sad. I was sure she missed me, but at least she was on a plane to Athens where everything was exciting and new. I had to return to the empty nest. Twigs and a couple of feathers were all that remained.

    I saw my reflection in the full-length mirror. The look of panic and rage in my eyes scared me. I started screaming, "Why did I let her go? Why did I let her go?" I knew only then that it wasn't good for me to have Celeste gone that long. Maybe only another parent could understand that. I stomped around the room for an hour or so, cried a lot, and went to bed feeling like an exhausted, defeated, old man.

    As I lay in bed, I prayed for help. Powerless over my daughter, powerless over my feelings, afraid of what I might do, sick and tired of the rage within me—I felt that my entire existence had taken the shape of a fist. Overpowered, defeated, alone, sweaty, humiliated, and with my stomach in my throat—I howled with my mouth closed, sounding like a wolf trapped in the back of a long, dark cave. Frightened. Forgotten. Thirsty. I felt the numbness, the fog coming on like Novocain. I closed my eyes and began to pray:

"Dear God, save me from this numbness. These feelings are horrible, but at least they are my feelings. Why, dear Lord, must I be knocked down so hard and so often before I will turn to you? Please let me rise up and kick this world in the ass! I don't want to lie here like a crippled boy. I hate that crippled boy within me. I hate him for his weakness! Why did I say 'yes' to every unreasonable demand my parents made? Why did I say 'yes' when they demanded my soul? Why didn't I stop my father in his tracks? Why didn't I punish them, or at least stand up to them? I want my hand wrapped around the throat of this world tonight! I want to go face-to-face with every person I ever said 'yes' to when what I wanted to say was 'no.' I want my daughter back! I never wanted her to go in the first place. But I wanted to have the approval of Celeste's mother. What do I have instead?

"I am lying in bed, in my underwear, crying, praying, admitting to you, dear Lord, that I am too weak to even sit up. Here I am, the big, tough guy. My face is scarred from hitting countless steering wheels. My bones are fractured from falling down endless flights of stairs. My teeth are crowned because the original ones rotted out of my head from years of neglect. I was once the arrogant drunk who knew how to rule the world, but couldn't feed himself soup, because the shakes drove the liquid from the spoon. I am the boy, the man, the drunk, the worker, the husband, the martyr, the father, the author, the lover, the loser, the weight-lifter, the dude. I am all of these selves, all equally powerless over other people.

"And so I'm moving very slowly on this prayer that leads to you, dear Lord, because I don't want to have to ask for help. But...please help me! I feel like life is killing me. So hard to cope. So overwhelming. Help me, dear Lord. Help me find a life worth waiting for, because this life I have tonight doesn't seem worth the bother. I don't want to implode. I'm too old to die young and full of potential. Being a father, I voluntarily relinquished my right to suicide. So please, help me regain my center. Bring me back to myself. Show me where faith lives. Lead me to grace. Do with me as you will. I hereby affirm my commitment to you, dear Lord. Reveal to me the next portion of the journey. I await direction. I am calming down. I understand. I have survived the wound and the world. These feelings will pass. I can rest now. Thy will be done, now and forever. Amen."

I woke up the following morning and went into the bathroom. I studied my image in the mirror and said, "Not bad." I picked up the pen and paper I keep in my bathroom for inspired doodlings and scribbled, "I have cried for two years straight now. There is no sign of letting up. How deep is this grief? Wow! I hope I will soon be purged of this sadness but, if not, it will be okay because I truly believe these tears are saving me from killing someone. And the one I am most likely to kill is myself."

I put down the pen, walked into the kitchen and paced the floor. It scares me when I write stuff like that. What else is inside me that is dying to get out? My writing arrives sometimes like bile, dredged up from some deep pit within me where my ancestors live. Sometimes I can feel them wandering around inside of me—five hundred years' worth of drunken Germans grumbling and wondering what in the hell I am doing to the family. My life is so weird. I wonder what it is about. Why am I here? I hope it is to write because, at the moment, that seems to be just about all I am capable of doing. That is not a true statement. I am actually capable of a lot more than that. I am capable of being a good parent.

Celeste is gone and I am alone. Being alone has allowed all these feelings to surface. The problem is not that Celeste is gone. The problem is that I am gone. I abandon myself when I get lonely. I walk the streets feeling hollow and dull. I miss Celeste but I am glad she is in Greece with her mother and future stepfather. She is enjoying a vacation that I could not provide for her. I feel frustrated and impotent that I don't have more money and time. I am tracking, but not acting on, this intense feeling of competition with them for the love of my daughter. I feel threatened with the loss of the love of my daughter because I don't have a plane ticket to Greece. That sounds so ridiculous, but the feeling is there. It's a small part of me, but the feeling is definitely there.

I am learning to take my own feelings into consideration. I have to be the one to tell myself that I deserve better. It sounds silly to me that now, in my late thirties, I am just learning to say no. My belief has always been that if I give in to everyone, then people will like me. The fact is that when I give in to everyone, many will take advantage of me.

I didn't know that I would react so strongly to Celeste's absence. The price of not stating my needs to my former wife was that my daughter was now gone for nine weeks at a time when I needed her with me. But I have been able to file the experience away as a painful lesson learned. I no longer wait around, hoping that people will feed me morsels of kindness. I am kind to myself. I ask for what I need. I stick to my conviction that I deserve what I need. I say no when I mean no.

The process of taking these actions frees me from anger at myself for getting into the situation in the first place. Making a mistake is fine as long as I take an action to correct it or reduce the possibility of it happening again. Getting off my butt and acting in my own defense, with respect, dignity, and humility, is what creates change. Through action comes freedom.

When Celeste was in Greece she had a wonderful time. I had a great summer without her. I enjoy being a father very much. I also enjoy very much my time without her. When Celeste returned she found a father who was a little taller—having grown in conviction and self-respect. And she found a father who was a little less powerless over his own feelings.

The Hope of Good Cape

I was offered, and accepted, an invitation to go visit Celeste on the Cape for a long weekend. I was invited to stay at Celeste's grandparents' home, but I inquired about a hotel. I eventually decided against staying in a hotel, although I thought it would be best for me. I cited my daughter as the reason. I wanted her to see that her father and her grandparents could get along. Everyone else she knows stays at the house. Why shouldn't her father?

I got off the train in Falmouth and Grandpa George was there to meet me with a kiss and a hug. It was late at night, and raining. The noise of silence hurt my ears. No train sounds, no Manhattan hum of electricity flowing through the veins of the city, no sound of countless tires on pavement to distract me. The fear of emptiness, of open spaces, began to fill me once again. The fear of change, my constant companion, whispered incessantly in my ear.

My daughter and Granny B. were asleep when we got home. I went to put my luggage away, and noticed a paper plate taped to my door with "Welcome Dad" written on it. I thought it was cute. I also thought Granny B. wrote it, not my daughter. Grandparents and teachers know what makes parents happy. I sneaked into my daughter's room and gave her a kiss and a tiny hug, so as not to wake her. There is nothing more innocent, more beautiful, more refreshing than the sight and smell of a sleeping child.

I went into the living room and began to chat with Grandpa George. We felt slightly awkward with each other. It had been four years and a failed marriage to his daughter since we had talked. I reached for a pile of snapshots lying on the coffee table. He beat me to them, and began handing them to me one by one, with a little narration accompanying each. All the photos he showed me testified to the fact that my daughter was having a wonderful summer with her "family."

I always feel as though I'm from a different species when I look at snapshots of "families." It feels as if I'm looking at a map of Mars, and am not quite sure if I am holding the picture upside down or not. I do not understand what "family" is. Is it a feeling? If you feel you are in one, are you in one? Is family an internal glow, a warmth, a tribal drum beating slowly and resonating in your chest? Is family a concept, a belief, a thought, a religion based on blood? I just looked "family" up in the dictionary, thinking how ridiculous it was that I had to do so. Imagine how you would feel if you had to look up "human being" in the dictionary to find out if you are one! When Grandpa George finished showing me the photos, I placed them neatly in a stack back on the coffee table exactly as I found them, which is the way I was trained to do things in a stranger's house. I noticed Grandpa George had a few photos left in his hands, which he discreetly placed on the shelf of a nearby bookcase. Then he said goodnight and went into his bedroom.

I went over and looked at the photos. No surprise. The photos were of my daughter, her mother, and her mother's fiancé frolicking on the beach. Giving credit where credit is due, I also thought it was sweet of Grandpa George to try to protect me. I was very pleased at how sensitive he was to how I might feel.

I felt a tinge of pain and discomfort at being in a place where I once, but no longer, belonged. I went to bed, thinking of how my former wife and her fiancé might have had sex on the bed where I was lying. No wonder I wanted to stay in a hotel. Lying on that bed made me feel creepy. I had had sex on that same bed with her. I couldn't remember what it felt like. I lay wrapped in a blanket of loneliness, a solitary cricket driving me crazy. I eventually fell asleep.

The next morning I was, as I always am, no matter where I sleep, the first one up. I got dressed and put on a long, black rain slicker over my clothes. I sat on the terrace, staring out into the wilderness. The last time I was on that terrace, I was the son-in-law of the residents. What does that make me now? A former somebody? Why is it that I seem to only have a definition in relation to other people? I seem to have to be somebody's something, or I fear I am nothing at all.

I heard the door to the terrace slide open. I turned to see my darling Celeste racing toward me, her bare feet slapping against the wet floor, arms outstretched, wearing white pajamas with teddy bears all over them, her messy blonde hair falling over her brown eyes, with a front toothless grin all for me! She was chanting "Daddy! Daddy! Daddy!" like a sacred mantra.

She sat on my lap. I listened intently as she gave me a tour of her inner world, full of rocks and fishing and science classes, swimming and newfound expressions, snatches of interpretations of overheard conversations between adults, titles of recently read children's books, a description of the world's best breakfast, and an urgent plea to know what we were going to do next, and what after that, and what after that!

We spent a wonderful day together.

We were sitting next to each other in the back seat of her grandparents' car during a long ride. Say something to her, I said to myself. The day is almost over and you have to go back to New York in the morning. I looked over to her. She looked at me, smiled a small smile, and looked back out the window again. I looked down at her tiny hand cupped in mine. This is truly love, I said to myself. Everything I have heard about it is true. All the clichés are true. All my daughter and I need from each other at this moment is to be together. We need no words. No events to attend. No promises. No bribes. No toys. Just each other.

That night we went to a dinner party in a spacious cottage overlooking the marina. The moored sailboats rocked gently in the rain like wet palace guards at the entrance to the sea. Celeste didn't want to share me with anyone. We sat on the porch and made up stories, while codfish swabbed in cumin baked in the oven and eccentric scientists spoke of Greek politicians and modern art. Four times that evening, I took Celeste for a walk in the rain.

In the car on the way home, Celeste reverted to about the age of four. Usually she acts like that when things are rapidly changing and she wants nothing to do with it. Sometimes she acts like that when she realizes she is getting older and is being handed additional responsibility for her own life. In other words, she acts younger than she is when she doesn't want to grow up. I indulge her during these times because I understand. I successfully delayed growing up until the age of thirty-seven.

We arrived home and I put Celeste in her pajamas. I read a bedtime story to her and rubbed her back until she fell asleep.

That night I had a horrible dream. I was at a cocktail party in a huge room on the twenty-eighth floor of a skyscraper. It was a rainy night and there were very strong winds. You could actually feel the building sway. That in itself didn't frighten me because I had heard of buildings swaying in strong winds before. But the building suddenly leaned very far, and a piece of furniture moved a little. At that moment I knew the building would not be able to right itself. The people stood frozen, mid-sentence, with drinks in their hands. Utter silence and disbelief preceded our destruction. I had thought there would be screaming. Maybe that was yet to come. I could hear the top of the building tearing off. It sounded like thunder. There was immense power in its roar. I thought of Celeste. Will she be killed? Will the building topple on her? No! She is nowhere near the building. She will live. I will perish. We will never see each other again.

So this is the way my life will end. I am calm. Like a reporter, like an artist, I record the feelings of my own death with awe and curiosity. The building top has torn off and is almost upside down, beginning its plunge toward earth. I expect to hear the screaming now. All denial about what is happening lies smashed on the floor, or is it the ceiling, along with the glasses, the mayonnaise, the Beluga speckled salmon canapes, the handbags, and the hope. I am going to die now.

"Daddy!" I woke to Celeste's voice, heard somewhere in the darkness.

"Daddy! Someone made my bed wet."

I opened my eyes and fumbled for the small light near my bed. Slowly she began to realize what had happened.

"I wet my bed," she said in disbelief, struggling with embarrassment.

"That's okay, honey," I said to her as I pulled her wet pajamas over her head and searched the foreign house for some clean ones. She held out a stuffed animal which I had just brought her the day before.

"I peed on Mr. Moose," she said with elephant tears welling up in her eyes. I thought quickly.

Well, you once threw up on Oinker, the stuffed pig, and he is okay," I said with great conviction. She felt better.

There was a spare bed in my room which I made up for her. I put her to bed, rubbed her back, and got back into my bed and turned out the light. We both lay in the darkness and tried, unsuccessfully, to sleep.

"Daddy," she whispered to me across the darkness, "promise me you won't go back to New York before I wake up."

"I promise."

She asked me to turn on the night light, which I did. My poor little sweetie finally sank into a shallow, furled-eyebrowed, closed-fisted sleep.

The next morning I sat again on the terrace wrapped in the black rain slicker. I tried to write about the experience I had the night before, but I was interrupted by Granny B. She brought me a cup of coffee and sat down.

I told her about what had happened with Celeste. She blamed it on the weather. I told her that it was rainy and humid for me too, but I didn't wet MY bed. I asked her if she had wet hers. She got my point. We had a nice talk and I realized that, although we were separated by four years and my divorce from her daughter, we still cared a lot for each other. More than for my sake, I was very pleased that I was getting along with my daughter's grandparents.

Celeste came out on the terrace and appeared emotionally hung over from the night before. We went for brunch at a restaurant at the foot of a drawbridge. Boats passed by, but Celeste's fear of my leaving didn't. Celeste was not interested in the boats. She wasn't even interested in strawberry pancakes. She just wanted to sit on my lap. Every five or ten minutes she would ask me, "Is it time for you to go yet?" When I answered no, she would relax a little.

We went home and I began to pack. She sat sullen and silent on the sofa. "I don't want you to go," she said, choking on her emotions, but at least she talked about her feelings.

I asked Granny B. if she thought I should stay a little longer. She said that no matter when I left, Celeste would be upset. She thought I had might as well go now, while Celeste was prepared for it. I asked to be left alone to think about it for a minute.

Being around my "former family" was very difficult for me. I was ready to bolt for the door and get out of there. I must also confide to you that there was a pretty woman back in New York who was expecting me to call that night. I felt guilty that my motives were not "pure" in wanting to go immediately back to New York. But, you see, I am sometimes a lonely man, in addition to being a good father. I kept thinking about what Celeste wanted and what was best for Celeste. Then an almost totally foreign concept entered my mind. "Wait a minute," I said to myself. "What about what I want for myself? What about what is good for ME?"

I told Celeste I wanted to stay for another six hours. That was the time at which the next train left. She was ecstatic! We went to visit a family that morning and had a lot of fun. We went to the fair held by the science school Celeste attended. We visited Grandpa's laboratory. We did all sorts of things that really didn't matter, as long as we were together.

It came time for me to leave. Granny B., Grandpa George, and Celeste drove me to the train station. Celeste had no problem separating from me. Those few extra hours had made all the difference. I had gone a little out of my way for her. She had gotten what she needed. I had given what I had to give, yet I still had plenty left for myself.

Please Tell Me What I'm Feeling

I said it the day she was born and I will say it now: Celeste does not belong to me. She is in my care, but her life is her own. I remind myself of this constantly, so that I may remain flexible and non-controlling. My trip to Cape Cod was an exercise in letting go.

I have to let go of my fear that I will die if something happens to my daughter. What if she drowns up there? What if she gets killed by a drunk driver? What if? What if? I am not consciously aware of being motivated to do good things by fear of bad things happening. But the presence of that fear would certainly explain some of my desperate feelings. My daughter, you see, is my primary relationship. She is my connection to "family." She is my connection to love. I fear that she will be snatched from me, like everything else I have ever loved. I do not let that fear interfere in Celeste's life. I do not make her stay home with me to still my worries. But I have sat with these haunting feelings since the moment she left.

When I returned from the Cape, my daughter was fine. She went on with her life. It was her father who got stuck. I must accept that the weekend really wasn't so much about Celeste as it was about my parents. Feeling like an outsider at my daughter's grandparents' house was exactly the way I felt as a child in my own home.

My fear of losing Celeste is really a fear of losing my parents, which is really a fear of losing myself. That explains why I came home from Cape Cod with a hole in my heart big enough for a snowmobile to plow through. Unless I let other people into my heart, it may be true that I couldn't live if something happened to my daughter. It is very dangerous for my daughter to be all the love I allow myself to know.

I think I am in danger of trying to protect my daughter from MY demons, not hers. I don't want to place my eyes in my daughter's head. I don't want her to have to see what she knows nothing about, and need know nothing about. She doesn't understand why her father is so very careful with everything. I'm glad she doesn't understand. She is leading a better life than I had as a child.

Celeste's version of my trip to Cape Cod is probably something like this: He arrived. We played. He left. I miss him. But I will see him in three weeks. My version, as you can see, is somewhat different.

It is time for me to accept my powerlessness over my daughter's destiny and to focus more on my own. It is time for me to embrace my own life. I feel better about myself. I feel better about my daughter.

Forced Labor

My daughter and her friend were sitting in a puddle near the shore on the beach at Cape Cod. I was with a group of adults nearby. I noticed the two children were sitting with their backs to each other. I have learned to recognize this affliction from miles away. It's called pouting.

I walked over, knelt down, and asked the children what the problem was.

"She won't talk to me," my daughter said with anguish.

"Is that true?" I asked the other little girl.

She nodded her head yes, without looking up at me.

"She has a right to be silent for a moment," I told my daughter.

"No, she doesn't!" my daughter exclaimed.

"Why?" I asked.

"Because," my daughter said, "I told her to talk about her feelings and she just won't!"

"That's okay if she doesn't want to talk about her feelings right now," I said soothingly.

The little girl was still staring at two mounds of wet sand, under which she had buried her feet. I could tell she was enjoying all the attention. She didn't even have to do anything for it, except remain silent and uninvolved.

"No, it's not okay if she doesn't talk to me about her feelings," my daughter said to me, "because I told her that if she doesn't talk about her feelings, she is going to grow up and have to write books about it like you do."

No Guarantee

I got home from work on a hot, summer night. The red light was blinking on my answering machine, signaling that I had a message waiting for me. I rewound the tape and played back the following message from my daughter, who was staying for the summer with her mother's parents on Cape Cod:

Hi, Dad, this is Celeste.
They killed John Lennon and he was famous.
You're famous too!
Please call me!
I love you! I love you! I love you!
'Bye.

Now what am I to do with that? And on what level am I to approach it? She knows that my second book, *Forgiving Our Parents,* is dedicated to John Lennon. Now that she is almost eight, she has an increased awareness of how dangerous New York City is. She is clearly scared and lonely being on the Cape without either parent.

And I cannot guarantee her that I will not die. I think that is what she is looking for. I think she wants me to be God. Perhaps I still am God to her, but I don't think so. That's the problem. I am becoming human. I am not as powerful as she once suspected. Nobody else is either. So she is losing her sense of safety. I think it is the seeming randomness of death and loss that is confusing her at the moment. I'm not sure. I do know that Celeste is remarkably good at talking about her feelings. I also know that she is, after all, only seven years old.

I find this the perfect time to talk to her about God. I call her every night at bedtime, at her request. I cannot tell her that I will not die. I can, however, tell her the truth. I can tell her that I believe God needs both of us on earth right now to do His will. We are also healthy, young, and strong. I tell her about how I let go of fear and beckon faith. She has a hard time doing that. So do I. I admit to her that my faith is not perfect. I admit to her that I am not perfect. She can accept that. I don't need to protect her from the truth. I only need to phrase it in a gentle, loving, and affirmative way.

Troubleshooter

A boy in Celeste's second grade summer school class at Cape Cod had a birthday party. I dropped her off at the party and came back to pick her up later in the afternoon. When I arrived, there was a live band playing. There was lots of food and drink. Children were singing and dancing. Adults were milling around and laughing. I was sorry I had missed it.

I found Celeste. She was dressed up like an Indian princess. The birthday boy came sauntering up to us. He had long hair, grown down over his ears. He was wearing a cowboy hat and had chaps over his jeans. He had on cowboy boots with spurs on the back of them. He was twirling his two pistols around both index fingers at the same time. He was wearing a brown leather vest over a bare chest. A face painter had been hired for the party, and the birthday boy had her paint CELESTE on both of his forearms.

Oh, no! I said to myself. This kid is exactly what I was like when I was little. I could have had Future Sociopaths of America tattooed on my forehead. And this kid had a crush on my daughter.

A while later we said goodbye and left. On the way home, I asked Celeste what that kid was like.

"Oh, he's into the usual things," she said.

"Like what?" I asked.

"Like sex and pickpocketing," she replied flatly.

She refused to elaborate. I didn't press her for an answer. Celeste hadn't spent much time with him. I figured there wasn't much point in upsetting her. I could always ask the teacher instead. This is a very expensive private school, mind you. This is part of what I get for my money.

You can't stop a kid from being a kid. Neither of the two children were doing anything wrong. I just want to satisfy my desire and right to know what my daughter is up to.

I have a deep suspicion that personality is hereditary. So is the tendency to create certain kinds of relationships. Children don't get much more troubled than I was, so I find this situation interesting. I think Celeste senses that her friend is a troubled boy, but she seems to want to stay clear of him. Not because he is a troubled boy. But because she is simply not attracted to the troubling issues that he speaks about and that his behavior exhibits. Very interesting. The difference between the way I was raised and the way I am raising Celeste seems to be having an effect on her personality, behavior, and choices.

I like the boy more than she does. He is very similar to the boy who exists, to this day, within me. Celeste, in the meantime, has developed a crush on what I would call a Future Really Good Guy of America. Instead of being into sex and pickpocketing, he is into science experiments and being able to spell "antidisestablishmentarianism" backwards.

It sure is funny how I don't want Celeste to go near the boy who is exactly like I was as a kid, and am happy that she is attracted to the kid I can't stand. I think Celeste is going to be all right.

That Daring Young Man on the Flying Trapeze

I sat on a bench at the foot of the trapeze for a week during our vacation, watching one after another brave beginner climb the narrow ladder to the summit of their fears. I even sat on the bench at night and watched the silent, sleeping monolith of a trapeze, hoping that this would somehow make it seem less terrifying.

My daughter had already been on the trapeze twice. There it was again, the glaring difference between my daughter and me. She had climbed up the scary ladder, swung out on the bar, hung upside down, released her hands, and fallen into the net with about as much fear and stress as is involved in brushing her teeth.

The lesson once again was clear. Excessive fear and negativity are learned. The lessons begin early in life. I used to think that fear was a natural state of being. I thought it was the common denominator of all people. It certainly was for me. Fear was my home, and I didn't question it any more than I questioned air.

I try not to communicate fear as a way of life to my daughter. Strangely enough, my daughter was taught courage, trust, and positiveness by an often untrusting, fearful, and negative father. How this bizarre twist occurred is beyond me. But I do know that children learn courage by watching their parents behave courageously. It doesn't matter that my daughter sees me being afraid. I don't try to hide that from her. It is quite important, however, that my daughter sees me struggling to overcome my fear.

I strapped on my belt and took my place in line. My daughter was playing soccer in a distant field and saw me get in line to go on the trapeze. She came running across the field to sit beside me and watch.

"Climbing the ladder is the worst part," she said. "The rest is easy. But the ladder is very, very, very scary!"

"Thanks, Celeste," I said, grateful for her support.

My eyes followed the ladder up to the top. I wondered if the little pouch tied to the pole up there next to the platform held enough rosin to dry my trembling, sweaty, cold hands. I was sweating so much I could imagine the rosin turning to cookie dough on my hands. I imagined my hands slipping off the bar and me falling, terrified and humiliated, into the net.

Despite my fear, my number was up. I had run out of excuses. My time had come. I knew I had to go through with it this time. If I failed to go up there, I would leave the island without having done what I feared and desired the most—to begin taking risks, and seeing that I could and would survive them.

The biggest fear was the loss of control. I could not control being terrified. I could not control what it would feel like to swing sixty feet out over a net forty feet below me. I could not predict what it would feel like to have my stomach flip up into my mouth. I could not control the experience by writing a short story about a trapeze and have it be a substitute for a trapeze.

In my drinking days it would have been different. I would simply have done it. I would have gone through the experience without any feelings attached to it. In my drinking days, there was no difference between dreaming about doing something and doing something. Numbness was the pillow I rested my life upon.

"Are you afraid of the trapeze?" the person next to me asked.

"I'm afraid of everything, but I do it anyway," I answered.

"Next," I heard. I suddenly felt like a prisoner waiting for the electric chair. My last thought before stepping onto the first rung of the ladder was, I am such a pro at making myself uncomfortable, I can't help but wonder if I am doing this to conquer fear, learn to take risks and have fun, or have I simply found a way to terrify myself on my vacation just to make sure I don't have TOO good a time?

Either way, I was climbing.

"Don't look down!" I reminded myself as I climbed the ladder that was as flimsy as a strand of spaghetti dangling from the fork of a wildly gesturing diner. I reached the platform and found it much narrower than my feet. I felt like a one-winged bird on a wire.

My mind flashed to earlier that day when I was beating the pants off of a macho man in a game of Ping-Pong. I thought he would be very upset if I beat him, so I let him win the game. I thought about how my subconscious had programmed me for defeat. I felt powerless over my need to lose. I climbed the ladder to the trapeze and felt the anger growing inside me as I realized what had happened to me. I wondered how many times, in how many different areas of my life, this self-defeating behavior had taken over, year after year after year.

Don't think. Your mind is your worst enemy at a time like this, I told myself as I climbed off the ladder and stood on the platform as the strong Caribbean breeze blew the fear off me.

"I bet you see lots and lots of people up here for the first time who are scared to death and feel it's too late to turn back, so I guess I might as well just relax and try to enjoy it, right? Huh?" I giggled and waited for some reassuring words from the man who handed me the bar.

"Place your left foot in the middle of the platform," he said as blandly as a taped voice announcing the store closing at Macy's. Hmmm. Suddenly my thoughts and feelings turned to just one thing: survival. I held on to the scaffold with one hand and the trapeze bar with the other. My heart was beating erratically and my head was filled with blood that was too scared to circulate.

One of the scariest things about the trapeze is how you leave the platform holding on to the bar with only one hand. The other end of the bar snaps almost immediately into your other hand, but the point remains that you step off the platform with the bar in only ONE HAND.

"Step!" he said and I obeyed the command to step off the platform. The other side of the bar did indeed swing over toward me as I had been informed it would. It was easy to grab with the other hand. At least I had the bar firmly in the grasp of TWO hands now.

"Legs!" I heard someone shout from the ground and I obeyed that command to swing my legs up through the space between my arms. I draped my legs over the bar.

"Hands!" I heard from the ground and I let go of the bar with my hands and hung upside down by my legs, my hands straight above my head, but reaching toward earth, like an inverted man under arrest.

Still swinging back and forth through the air, I bent at the waist, reached for the bar, and pulled my legs back down through the space between my arms until I was hanging straight down. The bar that had recently hurled me through space was now just gently swaying me back and forth, like a tired calypso marathon dance contest winner.

"Do you want to do it?" the voice from the ground asked me.

"Yeah!" I shouted.

"One. Two. Three. Release."

At that command I swung my legs forward, back, and forward again. Then I released the bar and did a somersault in midair before hitting the net.

Success! Triumph! Adrenalin!

I climbed down from the net and took a seat on the bench. My daughter came and sat beside me. I could tell she was proud of me and I could tell I was proud of myself.

I sat and watched a friend attempt his first time on the trapeze. We had both been too frightened to do the trapeze for six of the seven days we were on the island. When he saw me going toward the trapeze that day, he decided to try it too. His family, Celeste, and I all cheered him on. He did very well also.

As he and I walked away from the trapeze, I told him that going through with it had saved me $140. If I hadn't done it, I would have spent $70 with my therapist figuring out why I couldn't bring myself to do it. The following session, I would have spent another $70 figuring out how to evolve into a person who could go through with it the next time the opportunity presented itself. My friend told me that going on the trapeze took everything he had to offer. We had a bond of mutual understanding that didn't need words to solidify our feelings.

We both knew we had done something important.

Maybe someone who wasn't brought up in a traumatic family, as both of us were, wouldn't understand the extent of the fear that is the residue of such an upbringing. Maybe they wouldn't understand the dread of change, the avoidance of risk, the neutralizing of excitement. Maybe they would have no empathy for the agony of feeling unable to reach for your dreams, but dreaming nonetheless. Probably they wouldn't understand the feeling of not being entitled to success and competence.

But we understood.

An affirmation had taken place. The trapeze was nothing less than life itself, and we had expressed our willingness to participate, not passively and with only our intellects, but actively and with our whole beings. Strange, these little hinges upon which our lives turn.

In the midst of a crowd, with no one else knowing, my life had changed. My heart was beating in a new and stronger way. I slept well that night and dreamed I was at the circus, and everything was bright and fragrant and wonderful.

Coming Home to You

My daughter and I were vacationing in the Bahamas at a private club. The resort was on the Atlantic side of the island, and the water sports were conducted on the Caribbean side. There was a shuttle bus that took us from the club to the marina and back again. It was a very short ride. About five minutes.

    I decided one day that, rather than taking the bus, I would walk along the beach to the marina. I figured that a five-minute bus ride would roughly equal a half-hour walk. It was a sumptuous day. It was one in the afternoon and I had to pick up my daughter from a sand-castle-building contest at four o'clock. I reasoned that I would walk to the marina in about a half an hour, water ski for a couple of hours, take the shuttle bus back to the club, and still have twenty-five minutes to enjoy an espresso by the pool before picking up my daughter.

    I walked along the pink sand of the beach until I reached a rocky point of land. I carefully walked over the brief stretch of sharp rocks until I came upon another beach lined with a seemingly endless row of coconut trees. This was the distant Coconut Beach I had heard about at the club. Coconut Beach ended at a very rocky point of land which jetted several hundred feet out into the Atlantic Ocean. The island must have been made by a volcano. The rocks looked as if they had once been molten and bubbling crazily and then suddenly hardened to form sharp, needle-like, pointy spires about three to six inches high. The tops of these sharp spires snapped off under the weight of my sneakers, which were getting cut and scratched to pieces. I walked very carefully, thinking that if I fell on those rocks, my knees would be slashed to shreds. I didn't want to have to crawl home on bleeding knees.

I began to get a little frightened on that increasingly crazy walk. I attributed my fear to being a New York City slicker, who had learned to deal with beggars, thieves, and taxi drivers, but couldn't quite cope with endless pink beaches.

It was winter. The sun was hot. I had just arrived from New York the day before. I was the color of raw chicken, working on becoming lobster red. I was dizzy and parched. I threw a beach towel over my shoulders and head, and pretended I was Father Teresa on a pilgrimage to help the needy children of the primitive island learn to water ski. But I didn't see any children, or anyone else for that matter.

I looked at my watch. It was three o'clock. I had only a half-hour to get to the marina, and even then I would have to go straight to the shuttle bus to get back to the club in time to pick up my daughter. Forget about water skiing. I had to get back.

I made it around that volcanic obstacle course and was once again on serene, pink beaches. I looked back and told myself how lucky I was that I didn't have to go back the way I came, because I didn't think I could do it.

Where was the marina? It was almost time to go back, but I hadn't even arrived yet. I began to realize just how uninhabited the island was. I hadn't seen a house, path, or telephone line for almost the entire walk.

I looked up and saw yet another point of rocks. But before I could reach them, I came across a gully. It was too wide for me to jump across. It was too deep for me to jump into and then wade out of. I wondered if I could hang by the lip of the gully and drop into the shallow water on the floor of it. The drop would only be about two feet. But the floor was made up of rocks and there was water crashing over them. I was stumped. I climbed up the hill at the edge of the slanted beach and saw only jungle. I ran back down the hill and looked at the ocean, the width of the gully, the depth of the jump, and the ferocity of the waves.

I began to panic. I looked at my watch. My daughter was expecting me in thirty minutes. It took me two and a half hours to get to where I was. The marina was nowhere in sight. I couldn't possibly get back in thirty minutes if I went back the way I had come. I had to find the marina. It must surely be right around the next bend.

I crouched on the lip of the gully. I put my hands on the sharp rocks and began to prepare to lower myself into the gully and jump. Then a picture came into my mind. It was a picture of my daughter. I looked down at the slippery rocks and the waves crashing over them. One false move, one twist of the ankle, and I could fall and hit my head and bleed to death. Or I could be there for days. I could spend an enchanted evening on the beach with two broken legs and waves crashing over me. Then the thought struck me:

I must be nuts.

So what else is new?

I thought of my daughter on a Bahamian island waiting for a father who is lying dead on the beach. I had to turn back! I felt defeated and dejected, scared, angry, hopeless, and crazy. How do I get myself into these things? Why is my life always so nuts? All I tried to do was to go for a walk and I ended up in this existential nightmare.

I looked heavenward and shouted, "Okay God, what is it you want me to learn this time?" God knows I am a poor listener and must therefore receive my lessons in very loud, dramatic terms.

"What is the message you want me to know?" I asked.

"Go back," I heard.

"Go back? Is that it? Nothing deeper?"

"Go back. Return to your family."

"You mean my daughter?"

"Return to your family. You are not meant to be on this journey alone," I heard.

I don't want to get too mystical and scare all you good people off, but I have to tell you that God speaks to me in a very specific voice. It isn't a man's or a woman's voice because my God isn't a man or a woman. And what is more, God doesn't speak directly to me all that often. God usually speaks to me through people. Sometimes God speaks to me through events. But right before God is going to speak directly to me, I get this funny, fuzzy, very wide sort of feeling that I can't explain very well. All I can say is that, well, right before you are going to sneeze, you know it, right? Your eyes close. You take these short gasps. You reach for a tissue. There are certain behaviors and rituals that precede the event. Well, there is a very definite aura, mood, texture, and sensation that sweeps across me right before God speaks to me.

I was not particularly in the mood to receive an unwelcome lesson from God as I was going crazy on that beach. And I was not in the mood to have a conversation with anyone, including God, so I folded up my antenna, turned off my receptors, and refused to listen.

I ran down the beach, landing heavily on the footprints I swore I would never see again. "I've got to get to my daughter! I've got to get to my daughter!" I kept saying to myself over and over again as if it were my mantra. It was as if the sun were my caffeine and my adrenalin as heat fumes rippled their way up from the hot, pink sand. I was sunburned and thirsty, tired and scared.

I kept thinking of my daughter sitting alone on the beach with a sand bucket and shovel, looking for her daddy. I felt so immensely sorry for her. I didn't want her to have to worry. "I'm coming! I'm coming!" I kept saying to her, as if she could hear me.

I stopped to walk for a while. I was so winded and parched I could barely breathe. My mouth was filled with salty ocean mist mixed with sand dust. I knew my daughter was with some instructors and other children. They wouldn't leave her alone on the beach and I knew it. So what was the origin of my panic? Why hadn't I turned back long ago? Why was I unable to let go of even my most ridiculous intentions?

I felt so alone. I felt so abandonable. I remembered that when I was a kid, every time my parents walked away from me, I wondered if they were coming back. As an adult, with very little respect for myself, every time the going got rough I walked away from myself and wondered if I would ever learn to act in my own defense.

Trudging up that beach I realized that I want to have a sense of home. I want to learn to trust. I want to learn to not be so addicted to danger and I want to be able to return home without feeling defeated for doing so. I want to be able to retreat without it feeling like defeat. I would like to learn that it is sometimes appropriate to give in to fear.

I would like to do the same thing two times in a row without feeling that I am wasting my life in repetition. I hope for two years of my life in a row that seem at least remotely related to each other. I want to be able to ask for help and direction. I want to learn to sit with boredom for a while. I would like to meet new people on my journey and I want to be able to go for a walk on the beach without it becoming an event.

I started to run again. This time it was a quick, light run. I enjoyed it. I went past places where, just an hour before, I had taken slow, careful, fearful steps. I bounded across them like a young goat on a hillside. I came to the place where I had expressed gratitude that I would never have to pass that way again, and then I DID—laughingly—pass that way again. A tremendous strength was in me and I didn't know where it came from. But I knew I had it. What had taken me two and a half hours in one direction took me thirty minutes in the other.

It was five minutes after four. The sandcastle-building contest had started a little late, so all the children were still there. I found my daughter. She was a beautiful mess of tangled curls in her hair and chocolate in the corners of her mouth. A wet beach towel was thrown over her shoulder and was dragging in the sand behind her. The blue of the ocean was reflected in her eyes, and the radiance of limitless fun was reflected in her relaxed face. I felt as if I had just returned from the dead. With the detachment of a painter sitting on a lawn chair under an umbrella with brush and palate in hand, I watched the children play.

My journey was too personal to mention, let alone too crazy to believe. So I kept my mouth shut about it. Some experiences are best savored when kept to yourself.

I did, however, casually mention to one of my daughter's instructors that I had attempted to walk to the marina by following the beach, and I was surprised at how far away it was. I told her how I had to turn back when I ran out of time.

"I'm glad you did," she said, "because it would have been a few days walk."

"But it only took the shuttle bus five minutes," I said.

"That's because the shuttle bus goes across the narrowest point of the island. It is only three miles wide at that point, but it is a very long island. To walk around the island is about one hundred and fifty miles."

I looked heavenward with a much different expression than I had earlier in the day. I would probably still be walking if I had not come to that gully, and with it the realization that sometimes the best way to go forward is to be willing to look back.

Can You Hear the Ocean?

Two hours before we were to leave our Bahamian Island vacation, my seven-year-old daughter was getting dressed and I was in the shower. I heard crying and shrieking! I ran out of the shower to see what was the matter. It took me a few minutes to calm Celeste down enough to get her to talk and make sense.

"My ear!"

"What about your ear?"

It turned out that Celeste had found a tiny sea shell on the pink beach of that idyllic island.

"I held a large shell up to my ear and heard the ocean. I wanted to know if I could hear the ocean in the tiny one as well," she sobbed.

The shell got caught 'way inside her ear and wouldn't come out. We walked slowly to the office of the scuba nurse of the club where we had been for a week. She said that without a special tweezers with a light attached, she wouldn't dare prod around in her ear for fear of hurting the ear drum. She said she would try to reach the island doctor but, since it was Christmas Eve, she doubted he could be reached. She was right. She tried up until the time when we had to catch our flight. By then, I had been begging for two hours:

"Listen, nurse, you've got to get in touch with him! It's just a tiny little shell. I'm not asking him to perform brain surgery. Please! Don't make me go back to New York City and spend seven hours in a Manhattan hospital emergency room on Christmas Eve at midnight with a seven-year-old girl!"

No luck. The nurse gave us two plastic cups filled with cotton balls for Celeste to wear over her ears during takeoff and landing, so as to avoid the pressure build-up in her middle ear, which could cause swelling and puncture the eardrum. Celeste thought she looked ridiculous sitting in the cabin of the plane holding those plastic cups over her ears. She was dead right.

The joyous trip of returning to New York City on Christmas Eve all suntanned with sandy, wet beach towels in our suitcases was somewhat daunted by the specter of the fate that awaited us. I hoped they didn't have a Santa Claus or Christmas tree in the emergency room waiting area, which would be really macabre.

I stood up to get our luggage out of the overhead compartment and I heard Celeste say, "Daddy! Look!"

With my hands above my head, struggling with a reluctant suitcase in the luggage compartment, I looked down over my left shoulder to see Celeste smiling and balancing a tiny shell on the end of her index finger. It had fallen out all by itself.

"Well," I said to her, "could you hear the ocean in the tiny shell, or not?"

A Beautiful Day to Torment a Child

Sundays have always been rough for me, especially since my marriage broke up. Sundays have always felt like family days and I don't have a family, even though I long for one. So there is an edge, a sadness, a loneliness that is triggered in me every seventh day. The depth of my neediness sometimes makes me feel desperate for someone to talk to, to walk with, to care for and be cared for by.

It was what the weather reports referred to as "unseasonably warm," so my five-year-old daughter and I went into Central Park to celebrate the spring in winter. We paused near the Alice in Wonderland statue to listen to an obese, Charlie Chaplinesque violinist play "The Rites of Spring."

I got up my courage and sat down next to a young, attractive woman whom I had been watching while she watched the violinist. I can barely remember what she looked like, except that the color of her eyes matched the color of the water in the reflecting pool she sat next to. Oh, yes! I remember the sun glistening on her lips. I almost forgot about her auburn hair, thick, shiny, and freshly cut. And her hands, long and thin with one broken nail. And her arms, cradled around her knees, that were pulled against her chest. She had a graceful, calm energy about her.

We began to talk about—what else?—the weather. Then we talked about the characters—the violinist included—who returned year after year to Central Park. We began to talk faster as our excitement for each other grew. At least that is the way it felt to me. Who knows what she was feeling?

I was about to find out, though, when suddenly I heard, "Daddy. I want to go. Daddy! Let's go!" At first my heart began to sink. I wondered if I could get away with pretending not to have heard it. No way. I began to panic. I think I would have rather heard from the Grim Reaper. I tried to dissuade her once or twice. But it became obvious that she was not going to ease up. I thought about asking this woman for her telephone number, but it was just too soon. Maybe if I had five more minutes to talk to her it would have seemed appropriate. Maybe. Maybe. Maybe. Celeste moaned and pouted and pulled on my heartstrings once more. I turned and said to Ms. Nearmiss, "Good-bye. Nice talking to you." Celeste and I abruptly departed for some damn playground.

I was hurt and angry at being pulled away from that young apparition, that thin connection to the human race, that rare hope of being cared for by someone. I became furious with Celeste, although at the time I didn't know it. I blamed God—although at the time I didn't know that either—for sending me a lovely woman for thirty seconds so I could leave the park even more lonely and frustrated than when I arrived. For the rest of the day, I thought I might run into her once more. I rehearsed my lines for the time when we would meet again. But, a little further within me, I realized that this is New York and you take an opportunity the instant it comes along or lose it forever.

I found myself being mean to Celeste. Sometimes I was overtly mean to her, saying things like, "Get over here right now or you're going to get it on the fanny," in response to some minor transgression. Sometimes I was passively mean to her—withholding love, being cold and quiet, walking nine steps in front of her, wishing I was alone and knowing she could pick up on that.

After I had been emotionally distant from her for about two hours, we sat down to share an apple juice. We had left the park on that glorious first day of spring and Celeste was saying, "I don't ever ever ever want to go back there again."

We were on the steps of the Frick Museum and I said, "There is something I want to talk to you about."

"I know what it is," she said.

"You do?" I asked, at once curious and apprehensive about her answer.

"You want to talk about what you did in the park," she said.

"What did I do in the park?"

"You hurt my feelings," she sobbed, holding back a gargantuan cry.

At that convenient moment she spilled the apple juice and we walked to the store to get another. When we returned to the museum steps we both were in a lighter mood. I could tell communication was now possible. Although my daughter is only five and a half, I decided to risk being honest about what was going on in me.

I told her that I'd recently had a series of disappointments. Publication of my book had been put on hold. I was upset with my parents. I told her I was angry with her mother and I explained the situation a little bit. I told her I had a lot of problems that had not been resolved yet. I let her in on my life without immersing her in conversation she was not able to comprehend. I told her one more problem of mine.

"I'm lonely," I said.

"But I'm here with you," she said in a tone so sincere and loving I almost collapsed on the pavement.

"And I'm very, very grateful for that," I said. "But you know when you are around adults all the time and you sometimes get lonely for the company of another child?"

"Uh-huh," she nodded, eager to understand.

"Well, I'm lonely for the company of another adult," I said.

I was unsure at this point whether I was being inappropriate in including Celeste in some of the issues behind my behavior. I felt strange talking to my daughter about intimacy issues concerning myself and a woman. It reminded me of when I was a child and my mother would speak to me like I was her shrink or her best friend. It made me feel that she was out of control and therefore I was in danger. But this felt different. There was an expression of recognition and empathy on Celeste's face. My mother was out of control; I am not.

"I was very happy when I met that woman by the Alice in Wonderland statue," I continued, "and I wanted to be her friend. But you got upset and insisted that we leave. That made me a little sad and angry. Don't you want me to be her friend?"

"I don't mind if you're her friend," she replied.

"The why were you so upset?" I asked.

"Because you weren't talking to me."

"Next time I will be sure to include you in the conversation," I said.

Celeste felt abandoned by me when I turned my attention to the new acquaintance. It wasn't that she absolutely did not want me to connect with another person. The issue was that she didn't want me to leave her in order to do so. It was a matter of me including her in my life when I am with her. Had I allowed my daughter to talk to the woman as well, things might have been different. But then again, they might not have. Chance encounters are merely chance encounters. Brief conversations in the park do not always lead to romance, thank God.

Perhaps a more accurate title for this piece would be "A Beautiful Day to Torment Myself." Have you noticed how I manage to blame myself for things not going the way I think they should? My daughter pulls me away from someone I'm talking to and somehow I manage to make it all my fault. I am a blame-collector. Every interaction between me and another person that doesn't work out is because of something I said or did. Only when everything is right can I absolve myself of blame for it being wrong.

I often consider it my responsibility to "fix" my daughter so that she will never feel uncomfortable. I think this stems from some residual guilt about my wife and I splitting up. In some ways I feel that one way of making it up to Celeste for her broken home is to provide her with my undivided attention. I dote on my daughter. I rarely date women. Sometimes I feel as if I am remaining loyal to a family that no longer exists. I feel guilty that I'm not perfect. I feel angry that my best wasn't good enough. And I feel bad that my best attempts to guarantee that Celeste would have two parents who stayed together failed. So I have tried to be everything and everybody for her. What an awesome responsibility! I have become exhausted and frustrated and lonely. Celeste never asked me to do this. She only asked me to stay with her in the park.

I did not have a problem with my daughter that day. I had a problem with myself. My daughter split me apart from the competition. I let her do it. Such was my need to keep peace with my daughter. The name of my game is "Peace at Any Price"! But it backfired. I walked away from the possibility of having the female companionship I needed. Celeste wanted her daddy all to herself. And she got him.

What I got for going along with it was fury. I voluntarily subjugated my needs to Celeste's. That has been my lifelong role with everyone. "You First" is the name of my second favorite game. I play that game with lovers and bosses and family and friends. No matter who the person is, the lesson remains the same.

I must take care of myself first. Celeste and I were on a plane recently. The flight attendant was going through her pre-takeoff spiel. I listened very closely as she explained the use of emergency oxygen. "If you are traveling with a small child, place the oxygen mask over your face FIRST so that you may better assist the child."

How simple. How logical. If I am suffocating myself because I am not tending to my own needs, how can I ever expect to give appropriate assistance to another person?

I will take Celeste's advice and include her in conversations I am having with other people, so as to make her feel comfortable and not left out. I know what it's like to be a child and feel left out. But the next time I am in a situation like that, I will probably inform Celeste that I am busy talking to someone and I intend to continue doing so. I will explain that when the conversation is over I will take her to the playground. That way we both get a chance. There is plenty of life for everyone. I can't wait for anyone, especially a child, to give me permission to take my share, to live my life as I see fit. I will respect myself for that and, although Celeste may still want me all to herself, she will benefit from seeing her father treat himself with benevolent self-respect.

It sure is too bad that life's lessons, those beautiful gifts, are so often wrapped in pain. But how else would I get myself to sit down and think it through and find out what is behind my failures and disappointments, so that I may learn how to change and become more comfortable as a person and a parent? Sometimes gifts come in strange packages. I am sorry the woman in the park is gone. It would have been fun to get to know her. But without failing to connect with her, I wouldn't have had the opportunity to learn all this. She was a great teacher.

Single Parent Nightmare

I was in the restaurant where I have been the maitre d' for six years. It was the busiest day in the history of the restaurant. And I got sick. Very sick. I had to leave the dining room in the middle of lunch in order to lie down on the desk in the office. I never went back into the dining room that day. I stayed in the office. It took me an hour just to get the strength to change my clothes and try to make it home. It is impossible to find a taxi in midtown Manhattan at rush hour, and I didn't think I had the strength to walk to the bus, let alone ride on it.

The worst part was that I had to pick up my kid. Feeling like that, and having to go pick up an eight-year-old, was a single parent nightmare. There is virtually no way to prepare for a situation like that.

My daughter was having a play date with her friend because school was closed for a holiday. The mother of my daughter's friend informed me that Celeste had thrown up shortly before I arrived. Celeste was sick also. I offered to clean up the mess, but the mother had already done it. A lot of mothers are like that. She was very good to my daughter, as my daughter later informed me.

We stumbled out the door together, looking like two bowling pins with stocking caps on. It was freezing out. I was so sick my skin hurt. I felt like I was walking around inside a wet Brillo pad. We finally got a taxi and had him stop at a restaurant so we could pick up two cups of hot soup to go, which, when we got home, we discovered we were too sick to eat.

I got Celeste cleaned up and into her pajamas. I felt white and weak and sore and ready to faint the entire time I was getting her ready for bed. She finally went to sleep, moaning and breathing heavily. I crawled into bed, too weak to go into the other room to turn out the lights.

I have been sicker. But I have never been so miserable. I felt like a sick child with a sick child. At my weakest point, when I had virtually no strength to offer anyone, let alone myself, I had to take care of a sick child. There was no one I was close enough to to call for help. I was sick. And lonely. And scared. And cold. I wanted someone to cuddle me. I wanted some help with my daughter. I wanted to know it would be all right. I allowed myself to feel what a damn drag it is sometimes to raise a kid alone.

Sick Kid

I should be home, drunk, beating my kid. At least that is what the statistics say. Abused children of alcoholics grow up to be abusive alcoholic parents.

Instead, today I stayed home from work to nurture my sick daughter. I gave her medicine, cold baths, a ripe plum when she was feeling better. I read her books, talked to her, was there for her when she fell asleep and when she woke up.

She had fever dreams of blankets racing through the room. I turned on the fan and she hallucinated about it spraying bugs all over her. She screamed and tried frantically to brush them off. So I turned the fan off and fanned her instead with a book of rhymes.

She said she thought she was going to die. I promised her she wasn't and she said, "How do you know? What if God says 'Celeste, I want you dead'?" I talked to her about life and death, gradually changing the subject to playgrounds and stuffed animals, as her tired, milky eyes watched my lips form words she didn't understand.

I sat with her, running my fingers through her hair, watching her until her eyes closed and her breathing slowed and she fell into a comfortable, although feverish, sleep.

A memory of my own childhood cut through the gauze-wrapped years until it landed like a piece of contaminated food in the pit of my stomach. I remembered being a child, about my daughter's age, in a hospital in Japan, under observation for a mysterious leg disease. My parents checked me in. It was early afternoon. They left, saying they would return that night.

The sun set. I sat up in bed, looking through the window slats out onto a parking lot, watching for my parents' car, and sobbing. A kind nurse went off duty, and a cranky one came on. She reprimanded me for my sobbing many times. A few hours later she came in, snapped the window slats closed, and turned off the lights.

"Stop sobbing! Act your age! Your parents aren't coming, and even if they did, they wouldn't be allowed in. It's nine o'clock. Visiting hours are over. So stop crying and go to sleep!"

She left the room. I slid down in bed. I stuck a corner of the pillow into my mouth. It tasted like bleach and illness. It muffled the sounds as I cried myself to sleep.

I didn't walk for the next five years.

The memory and the feelings left me like fumes being sucked out of a restaurant kitchen. I looked down at my sleeping, sick child.

I am learning to love. I don't know where it is coming from. I was raised by troubled parents. I am the youngest child and a single, male parent with no previous experience with children. I have no spouse. All my love relationships have been seriously flawed.

And yet, somehow, despite what I have been through, I am learning to love. I love and nurture my daughter the way I was never loved and nurtured.

I am grateful. I am changing from the cold, hard, emotionally closed man I once was. I want to remember I said this. I am coming alive.

A Grieving Child with a Grieving Child

I tried to get some sleep the night my mother died. I didn't have much luck. I was up most of the night but did manage to sleep for one sweaty hour before I woke up early in the morning with a gooey coating of sadness all over me. I stumbled into the kitchen and made a cup of coffee. I stared at a spot on the kitchen floor for quite a while. There were no thoughts or sounds within me. I flicked through the channels in my brain and all of them were off the air. I decided to take a cold shower in hopes that that would bring some feeling back into my body.

The shower helped, but I felt that what I really needed was a bicycle ride. I got dressed and walked out the door, paused a moment, and walked back in to look for my favorite coat. I thought I had left it in my daughter's room. I walked into her room, grabbed my coat, and said good-bye to Celeste's pet hamster, Squeaker. I stopped, looked back, put my face next to the cage and yelled "Squeaker!" The hamster didn't move. I picked up one end of the cage and dropped it. Nothing happened. I dropped it once more. Nothing. I shouted again.

The hamster was dead! I tilted my head heavenward and shook my index finger at God. "Not funny!" I said. I looked another time at the hamster and then I fled the building. I got on my bicycle and peddled down the street as fast as I could.

I knew I needed help badly. I was stunned with disbelief. How could it be? What is happening here? What kind of a curse is this? Images began to flash through my mind at a frantic pace. My mother's death. The hamster's death. Ten hours apart? It can't be! Numbness wrapped me in its blanket. I was in the midst of tragedy and suddenly I couldn't feel a thing.

I went to my place of worship because I needed help in dealing with the loss of my mother. And I needed help in breaking the news to my daughter of her pet's death.

I sat in the office of the head of my place of worship with healthy tears streaming down my face. Thank God my feelings were returning. I feared the feelings of my mother's death, but I feared the pseudo-sanctuary of numbness even more. I recounted the horror of my previous ten hours to him. He listened to me for quite a while without comment or judgment, but with an aura of love and support.

He suggested that the loss of my mother and my daughter's hamster on the same day could possibly be a blessing. He said that my daughter's feelings about my mother's death could be very abstract, since my daughter had only met my mother once, two years earlier. But her feelings about her hamster's death were very real. Perhaps we could both learn about grieving together. Perhaps we could get through it together in ways that we could not get through it alone.

I had no idea what I was going to say to my daughter. Is there any "right" way of doing this sort of thing? I had allowed the hamster to lie in the cage exactly the way I found it a few hours earlier. I had heard of parents and teachers not removing rotten pumpkins from window ledges until the children came back from holiday so they could see the process of decay. I resisted the temptation to sweep death away from my daughter's life so as to spare her from aspects of life that I couldn't handle, and assumed she couldn't either. I resisted the temptation to have the prospect of a new hamster looming on the edge of mourning. Is there such a thing as an appropriate period of mourning before you replace the deceased with a new source of affection?

I stood in the stairwell one floor below my daughter's classroom, crying. There had been too much death. I was a child who had lost my mother and I had to pull myself into my parent mode in order to tell my daughter about the death of her pet. What a horrible task! How could I step aside from the black humor of this "coincidence" and not let my anger at the bizarre fate of two deaths in one day come to the surface?

I wiped my eyes and breathed deeply, hoping that deep breathing would keep me calm and centered. The grief was like a vacuum so strong it could tear the buttons off my shirt and suck the rings off of my fingers. I wanted to escape, to run, to get it over with. I wanted to find someone to do the work for me. Perhaps my ex-wife could bail me out of this one. Maybe I could lapse into the sensitive poet syndrome and someone could come to my emotional rescue.

And yet I wanted to do it "right" for my daughter. I wanted to be graceful and poetic and perfect. I wanted to shield my precious daughter from the sense of outrage and self-pity that lurked barely beneath my shiny facade of faith and fairness. How could I explain this to my daughter? What affirmations could I use to feign faith when I felt so shattered, angry, and lonely?

I struggled against the grief with all my might and it did not budge. I was in control of my emotions like a cartoon character trying desperately to close an overstuffed suitcase. My feelings would not yield to tyranny. I didn't know how to have feelings and be in control of my life at the same time. And it was certainly not appropriate to walk into my daughter's classroom crying. So much for trying to grieve gracefully. There was no easy way out.

I resorted to my old ally, numbness. There was such an aura of numbness about me when I walked into my daughter's room, I felt all the pencils would lose their sharpness, all the lights would dim, the laughter of the children would turn to stifled silence. I was the bearer of bad tidings. I felt as if I should be carrying a sickle and wearing a hooded, black robe. Instead of feeling as if I had experienced death, I felt as if death had experienced me. I felt like death itself coming to pick up my daughter at school.

Celeste was playing on the rooftop playground just beyond the sliding glass doors of her classroom. "Celeste, time to go home," I heard myself say. It was the day before the end of the school year and Celeste had cleaned out her closet. We carried home bags and bags full of clay duck families, paper hats, hand-written books, drawings, silly notes, bracelets made of macaroni—all the trappings of a successful second grade, all the signs of life, all the proud accomplishments of a happy little girl.

We got home and Celeste wanted to show me what she had collected during the entire year. She headed toward her room. I couldn't yet let her see the hamster. I stopped her with a shrill command, as if she were headed, unknowingly, toward a cliff. "Sit down," I gently directed her. I took her hands in mine and she sensed an ominous occasion. I said to her:

Ah, listen, Celeste. Last night I got home late and there was a message on my machine from my father saying that my mother had died.

C: What was his voice like?

Me: He was kinda scared. His voice was kinda shaky. And I have to go to Florida where my father still lives and where my mother died. I have to go there early tomorrow morning. Sorry. But I have to. Because something very serious has happened in the family. I am just going there overnight. It won't be a long trip. Is this okay so far?

C: Yeah. Were you crying?

Me: Yeah. I've been crying a lot. Why? Does that surprise you? You've never seen me cry, have you? You'll get a chance because it comes and goes. I feel okay, then I get sad, then I feel okay and I get sad again. Do you have any questions?

C: No. (Pause.) What are you going to do with her?

Me: You know there are two different ways to go when you die. You can get buried or you can be cremated. Do you know what cremated is?

C: Burned.

Me: Yes. My mother wants to be burned. So she is at the crematorium.

C: Are you going to see her being burned?

Me: No. But what I will do is—is to spread her ashes on the water so the waves can take her away and she can be with the water and the birds in the sky.

C: Was your dad there when she died?

Me: No. She died in a hospital. She died in no pain.
C: That's good.
Me: It's very good.
C: You said you had three things to tell me.
Me: Two things, honey. The other thing is going to upset you even more. (Pause.) Some things happen and you don't know why. And sometimes things happen all at once. I woke up this morning, Celeste, and I found that Squeaker was dead. I'm sorry honey.

There was a moment's pause, and then this wail spewed out of Celeste. It scared me. I had never seen such uncontrolled, spontaneous grief in my life. Her face was flushed red. Her nose was running. She was choking and coughing on her own saliva.

C: Where did you put him?
Me: I left Squeaker just the way he was. He's still there, in the cage.
C: Lying dead?
Me: Lying dead.
C: I don't want to go in my room.
Me: You don't have to, honey.
C: It's not fair! It's not! Why did he die? How old was he?
Me: One year.
C: That's it?
Me: Yeah.
C: It's not fair! I'm not going to be happy tomorrow. My Squeaker! I didn't get to say 'bye!
Me: You can still say 'bye.
C: No I can't. It's not fair. Why? Why did he die?
Me: I don't know, honey.
C: No! I'm not going to be happy. Even if you buy me a different pet. That's not fair.
Me: Squeaker was a lovely, wonderful hamster and you are a lovely, wonderful girl, and you're right. It's not fair.
C: I'm not going to be happy today. And not tomorrow. And not the day after.
Me: It's a very sad day.

C: I want Squeaker! I want Squeaker!

Me: I want Squeaker too.

C: I know! . . . Oh, no! I thought all of these days would be happy.

Me: They might be. We'll have to see.

C: Daddy!

Me: I'm right here, honey.

C: I want Squeaker.

Me: We'll always have a memory of Squeaker. Squeaker was a very special hamster.

C: I know. How did he die?

Me: I don't know.

C: How did you find out?

Me: I went into the room looking for my coat and I saw Squeaker and I had the feeling that he was dead.

C: How did you know? Did you knock on the cage?

Me: Yes.

C: And he didn't do anything?

Me: No. It seems so unfair, doesn't it?

C: Yes.

Me: And it hurts so much! Let it out, honey. Come on. Let the hurt out.

C: Did you tell Mommy?

Me: Yes, I did.

C: Did she say anything?

Me: She said that you are a very strong girl and I am a very strong man. And we will be sad together. And we will be strong together. . . . And we will get over this together.

C: I can't get over this tonight.

Me: No. Not tonight, honey.

C: I hate it.

Me: I hate it too.

C: I wish this day was happy.

Me: I wish this day was happy too.

C: I don't want to have to eat dinner.

Me: You don't have to eat dinner if you don't want to.

C: I thought this day was supposed to be happy.

Me: Life changes without letting us know.

C: It's so unfair.
Me: It's going to be fine.
C: I won't be fine.
Me: You will, honey, in time. But you don't have to worry about being fine now. Let your feelings come out.
C: I'm afraid to see Squeaker dead.
Me: You don't have to.
C: Then how am I supposed to go in my room?
Me: I'll remove Squeaker for you, but I wasn't sure how you felt.
C: Where will you put him?
Me: Well, I was thinking we should bury Squeaker.
C: Where?
Me: In the back yard or in the country.
C: Back yard where?
Me: Where the building used to be. We could dig a little hole.
C: No. It's ugly there. And they might build a new building there.
Me: How about the country? It's beautiful.
C: I won't be able to have any friends over to enjoy Squeaker. Not in my room. And I won't be able to sleep.
Me: I think all of that is true. But it will pass, honey.
C: How do you know?
Me: I know because I'm your dad. And I have lost my mother.
C: My hamster and your mother died at the same time? You found out this morning?
Me: Yes.
C: It's not fair.
Me: No, it's not.
C: Yeah, but what if we move to another country. We won't be able to see his grave.
Me: We're not moving anywhere.
C: When my friend Tyler comes over she won't be able to rattle the cage.
Me: That's true. She won't be able to rattle the cage.
C: Why did you have to tell me so many sad things?

Me: I really wish I didn't have to tell you so many sad things.

C: Especially all in one day.

Me: It's too much! Isn't it ridiculous?

C: (Pause.) I want to go see Squeaker.

Me: You want to?

C: Yeah. But I'll be crying so hard.

Me: That's okay. Tell me when you're ready.

C: I'm ready.

Me: Let's go.

We walked slowly, hand in hand, into her room. Celeste looked at the body of Squeaker and let out a stream of howls and screams the likes of which I never want to hear again. She hurled herself on her bed and began writhing and convulsing. This continued for a couple of minutes before she said:

C: He's not in the position that he sleeps in either.

Me: That's because he's not sleeping, Celeste.

C: Now I know he's dead. I want to die too! I want to die. Why Squeaker? Where are you going to put him? In a box?

Me: I thought I would put him in a little bag.

C: But then he will suffocate in there.

Me: He can't suffocate, Celeste. He's dead.

C: I know. But I was thinking he would suffocate if he was alive. I want to go.

We held hands and walked slowly out of the room. We sat back down at the kitchen table and, after a moment of bloated silence, I suggested we begin to plan the funeral.

C: Why didn't Squeaker just go to sleep and die? Maybe someone came in and killed him.

Me: No. Squeaker died because it was time for Squeaker to die.

C: No it wasn't! Sharon's hamsters both lived for three years! And ours wasn't even one year. (Pause.) I want to bury Squeaker in a quiet place—not in a playground.

Me: No. Near a tree.

C: Why?

Me: Trees are so strong and proud.

I felt as if I was going to explode into tears. Here I was, a grieving child trying to comfort a grieving child. I didn't feel comfortable doing that at all. Instead of exploding, I said:

Me: Go wash your face off and I will put Squeaker in the box. But first, let's write a note for Squeaker.

C: I'll say it and you write it.

Me: I'm ready.

I began to write with a trembling hand, as Celeste dictated:

Dear Squeaker,
I hope you had a happy life.
And I hope you will have a happy life in heaven.
Love,
Celeste and Dwight

Celeste didn't want to be in the room when I removed her pet's body from the cage and put it in the clear plastic, salad takeout container from the deli. I was afraid to touch Squeaker's stiff body, so I lifted the body with the small digging tools I had planned to use to make the grave. I am very glad that Celeste didn't see me in the throes of my fear of death and corpses, picking Squeaker up with a spatula and a gravy ladle.

Inside the see-through coffin, Squeaker reminded me of Cinderella, except that Cinderella didn't have fur all over her body. I placed the coffin inside a brown paper bag, to spare Celeste the sight of a stiff, awesome death. Then I placed that bag inside a petite Clinique bag with handles, along with the gravedigger tools. I was ready.

Squeaker's Funeral

With the note in my pocket, we grabbed our coats and left the apartment. Celeste was all right on the way to the park. We talked about things other than death, which was encouraging. Celeste didn't want to hold the bag with Squeaker in it, but she did want to hold my hand while I held the bag. I felt we were pallbearers in a two-person funeral procession.

We went into Central Park and found a plant, almost the shape of a tombstone, growing at the base of a large tree. I dug a hole while Celeste stood silently next to me.

"Well, I think this hole is deep enough now," I said.

Something dropped into the hole, and I leaned forward to peer in. There was a marble, lying in the moist dirt among the pale roots. Celeste stared into the pit at her marble.

"That's a lovely gift to give to Squeaker," I said to her. "Do you want me to put the note into the hole now?" She nodded yes. I placed the note in the grave, then lowered Squeaker's coffin into it. I filled the grave with dirt and packed it down. Then I scattered the extra dirt around the area, so that the freshly dug grave would not look like what it was and perhaps attract curious children. We said a prayer of thanks for all the fun times, and then we said good-bye. Celeste was solemn, but not crying, throughout the procedure.

But in our apartment, a couple of hours later, Celeste began to cry. She said there were rats in the park and she was afraid they were going to eat Squeaker's body. I assured her that Squeaker was untouchable in the plastic coffin and was very deep underground. That appeased her a little. Then she said she was upset about the wine bottle lying near the grave. I told her I would remove it.

I was worried about Celeste. The wild storms of tears and screaming were over, but a dull, deep sadness had set in. I felt so powerless to save her. And at the same time I didn't want to save her. I didn't want to replace the pet right away, in order to make the pain go away, and simultaneously give her the message that all forms of love and loss are avoidable or immediately fixable. But the hardest thing I have yet done with my daughter was to see her feel life torn away from her with no forewarning and no apparent reason. I watched a piece of innocence stripped away by the experience of death.

For the rest of the evening she remained calm, except for a couple of bouts of sobbing and struggling to understand the incomprehensible. I did not try to answer all her questions. I just let them hang there like underripe apples on a tree. After all, this was my first loss of a family member myself, and I was unprepared for the thousands of questions, images, jagged feelings, and pointed thoughts that swirled around my mind and heart.

The next morning, as I was brushing Celeste's hair and getting her ready for school, she stood staring at herself in the dressing mirror. She was calm, quiet, as sweet as always, and deeply engaged in thought.

"Does Squeaker still have hair?" she asked.

"What?"

"In the grave, does Squeaker still have hair?"

"Yes, Celeste," I answered. It takes quite a while for the hair and other parts of the body to begin to disappear after a burial."

"The bones are there for a long time, right?" she asked, and continued before I could answer. "I know the bones will be there for a long time because I believe in dinosaurs. They lived a long, long time ago but their bones are still here. I know because I've been to the Natural History Museum. I want Squeaker's bones to last until I am a grown-up."

"Why?"

"Because when I am a grown-up I am going to take my children to Central Park to meet my pet."

That night, after Celeste was asleep, I called her mother to brief her on what had happened and to make plans for Celeste, since I would be leaving for Florida at four in the morning to try to do the same thing for my mother that

Celeste and I had just done for our hamster. I told her what Celeste had told me about going to visit Squeaker with her children when she grows up.

"I bet she will," her mother said.

"What?"

"I bet she will take her children to see the grave where she and her father buried her first pet."

"I think you're right," I said. "I think you're right."

For both Celeste and me, Squeaker had been a great friend and a great teacher.

Burial at Sea

The day after Squeaker's funeral, I went to Florida for a couple of days. I saw two of my siblings I hadn't seen for twenty years, but there was no funeral for my mother, no coffin or flowers or minister or scripture or service. My father didn't want to be bothered with ritual, remembrance, and regret.

I was the one who offered to fulfill my mother's final request, that her ashes be spread on the ocean. No one else in the family wanted to deal with them. So now, a month later, having survived Penn Station in New York City on a hot summer Friday rush hour, I was on the train to Cape Cod with the brown plastic box containing my mother's ashes zipped into my suitcase.

I was traveling in the night with a box containing my mother on the way to visit my daughter, who was staying with my former in-laws. I spent the night with them, and the next day, before a scheduled book signing, I asked my former mother-in-law to drive me to a beautiful place where I could deposit the ashes in the ocean while she waited in the car.

Celeste didn't want to go. I honored her request that she go to the beach with her friends instead.

On a rock- and bush-covered nob of land in a nature sanctuary, slipping on wet, seaweedy rocks, nervously and unceremoniously I shook the bag into the ocean.

I had expected a cathartic event. Back in New York I had prepared my prayer that I was going to recite. I thought it would be a very spiritual and beautiful experience of letting go and moving on. I thought I would feel a sense of lightness and freedom. Instead, what I felt was terror!!

It was a very hot, clear July twenty-fifth in the middle of the afternoon, but the atmosphere at the site of the release of the ashes was so charged, I am surprised there wasn't lightning and thunder! There had been an intense aura of struggle going on. This was no an easy, serene rite of passage.

Damn, I said to myself as I walked away from the shore, I couldn't even do THAT right! Sorry, Mom. But I was really scared!

I went immediately to the bookstore and sat there for a couple of hours, talking and signing books, ever mindful not to press my wet sleeve against the pages. I didn't feel numb. I felt . . . stunned.

Celeste and I went to the beach later that day and I pretended to forget about what had happened, although my daughter sensed my sadness. "You're thinking about your mother, aren't you?" she asked me.

"Yes," I replied.

"That's good," she said. "Go ahead and think about her."

When I put my daughter to bed later that night, she asked me how it had gone.

"I was very frightened," I told her.

"I would have been too," she said, as she rolled over and went to sleep.

It was strange that only at that point did I realize that what I had done was a very courageous, loving, and scary thing. Even though it was "only" from the lips of a child that I heard it, I felt so validated by Celeste acknowledging the difficulty of what I was going through.

Everyone else was silent, unable to—or not seeing the need to—express support verbally. But I was rescued from a dark cavern of isolation by a seven-year-old girl saying, "I would have been scared too."

Squeaker's Grave Revisited

One of the things I did when I got back to New York was to go to Central Park and visit Squeaker's grave. There was not much to see. I kicked away the wine bottle that had bothered Celeste so much and cleaned up all the paper trash in the area. I said a few thoughtful, loving things to our dead hamster. And I thought to myself, Isn't this amazing. We can love and memorialize our pet rodent. We can give the hamster a decent burial, but we can't give my mother one.

Spooky

I hesitate to write this because you might think I made it up. But I didn't. I was putting Celeste to bed. I gave her a kiss goodnight. She took my face between her two hands, looked directly into my eyes and whispered, "Please don't tell anybody just how much older than you I really am. Goodnight." Then she kissed me and turned over and went to sleep.

Yikes! Sometimes Celeste scares me. If this is Celeste at seven, imagine her at seventeen? This vision is too bright and it hurts my eyes.

I guess doing my best and forgetting about the rest will have to suffice. Beyond prayer and effort, all that is left is faith.

Pervert or Not?

A boy, about ten, deemed old enough to go to school by himself on a New York City public bus, sat in the middle of the back seat. A strange person—I could not decide if this person was a man or a woman, or if this person was forty, fifty, or sixty—sat down next to the child.

The person began to speak to the child about petty things. The talk became incessant, although not offensive, except that the child had no interest in responding. The conversation, if you can call it that, went from the weather to increasingly personal things. Once again, nothing was rude, just a little peculiar. I watched the faces of the dozen or so people who could see or hear what was going on. No one paid attention. The person then asked the child what time he went to bed.

At that point I got up out of my seat and asked the boy if he wanted to change seats with me. He emphatically shook his head and silently mouthed the word "no." I sat back down, put my book away, and waited for a clearer opportunity to label the incident "abuse," so I could pull the child out of the situation. Nothing obscene or provocative was said. I could tell by the child's eyes that he was becoming increasingly frightened. But children are very self-conscious and hate to be caught in a scene. He desperately didn't want me to make him change his seat. He wanted to sit still, and wait for the incident to pass. I also wondered if the child thought that I was yet another weird adult who was on the scene to scare him.

The bus stop, fortunately, was directly in front of the school where I overheard the child say he was going. The child stood up and moved to the back door of the bus. The person stood up and moved to the back door of the bus. The child got off. The person got off. I did not get off, but I kept my gaze on the child, ready to get off at the next stop if I saw something suspicious. As the bus pulled away, I saw the child race into the door of the school, leaving the person shouting something after him. The kid was safe inside.

For the rest of my journey that morning, I thought of how there was a collective abandonment of that child by the adults who surrounded him on the bus. The person did nothing overtly wrong, but it was surely inappropriate to be asking such direct and personal questions of a child. The child was obviously scared, perhaps in danger. No one wanted to think, or feel, or be bothered.

The person, you see, had done no wrong. Nothing crude. Nothing overtly sexual. No hand was laid on the child. It was merely a case of a leering, crazy, looming eunuch moving in on a child on a public bus. No big deal. This is New York City. You have to expect things like that to happen here, right? The law would not have supported me if I had intervened and a scuffle ensued. And what if the person had a gun?

Was I simply projecting my childhood issues onto that child? As a child perpetually frozen by fear, I, too, sat silent and waited for the abuse to pass. I, too, was embarrassed by the craziness the attention caused. I, too, might have refused intervention, had it been offered. And besides, adults frequently play hide-and-seek and kootchie-koo with anonymous children in shopping centers and buses, don't they? Perhaps the other adults on the bus didn't respond because they were all from healthy families and weren't as sensitized to child abuse as I am. Perhaps everything was okay, and I was the only one who didn't know it. Who am I, after all, to jump in on a conversation on a public bus, uninvited, and label it "abuse"?

Self-doubt is the plague of my soul.

The important thing is that the child is safe. The child might learn a lesson by telling his parents and teacher about his experience on the bus. I hope so, then he and his friends can learn how to deal with similar situations in the future.

I might also learn a lesson about how a little abused child lives on within me. I have not resolved a lot of feelings surrounding issues from my past. I sometimes still feel that I am frozen on the back seat of a city bus and anyone can come up and dump their nonsense on me, and I have to sit there, be polite, and take it. I learned how I have not fully recovered from sitting and listening to drunken rantings, and feeling that I have no right to get up and move on, or to ask the person to be quiet.

I have learned how I sometimes will do anything, including suffering abuse, to keep negative attention from being focused on me. I learned on that bus how, as a child, I was unable to cry for help, and how other adults used that silence as an excuse to ignore the obvious peril of a helpless child.

But I also learned that I am not helpless anymore. I learned that I would, and did, stand up to abuse. I will defend myself and children the way I was not defended by my own parents. I need not sit idle, silent, or frightened and watch my life unravel in the hands of a stranger. I learned that I am on my own side, no matter who else is or is not on my side. I learned that I am my own son, and my own father.

The days of numbness and silence are over.

Forgiveness and Children

Adults who were children raised in dysfunctional family systems have a difficult, but certainly not impossible time letting go of past hurts and learning to parent the way they were never parented.

Celeste is much healthier than I was when I was her age. I am pleased to say that my daughter can't identify with what life was like for me as a child. She draws a complete emotional blank when she tries to understand the neglect and abuse that is rumored to have taken place in her father's childhood. I don't think anyone—child or adult—can truly understand neglect and abuse, on an emotional basis, unless he or she has lived through it. I have not divulged to my child the gory details of what my life was like as a child in a home where both parents were alcoholic. But my daughter does know what is perhaps the key issue, that I was not loved the way she is loved.

Celeste is a healthy child. The miracle of miracles is that, considering what my childhood was like, I have been able to become a successful parent even though I was never successfully parented. I learned very few healthy rules about bringing up children. But much to my surprise and delight, I have learned a lot about being a loving person and a parent from my daughter.

I was getting my daughter ready for school the other morning and she said to me, "Were your parents mean to you?"

"Yes, they were," I replied, surprised at this question that came, apparently, out of nowhere.

"Why?" she asked.

"Um . . . I'm not sure . . . I . . . uh . . . think they were mean because that is the way they were treated by their parents when THEY were little."

"Then it's really not their fault, is it?"

"No, I guess not," I replied.

That was the crux of the issue as far as my daughter was concerned. Something bad had happened to me as a child, and she had compassion for me to the best of her ability. But she was not overly concerned with who was to blame. She was more concerned with getting on with the repairs. It was as if she had a built-in emotional no-fault insurance policy.

It is not that my daughter has no feelings about abuse. I know that when she saw a child being verbally abused by a parent on a bus, she felt sorry for the child, was upset by the abusive language of the parent, and felt powerless to intervene on behalf of the child. She knew, intellectually, that her father's childhood was like that. She saw that the situation was bad, more so than the individuals in it. She didn't become fixated on the most negative interpretation of the relationship, the way her father did as a child, and sometimes still does. In other words, she didn't witness an abusive situation and immediately draw the conclusion that life is a horrible place, populated by horrible people who do horrible things to each other and therefore can't be trusted. She didn't feel the need to choose sides immediately. Nor did she feel compelled to abandon the "villain" and rescue the "victim." My daughter looks at an abusive situation, sees if there is anything redeeming that can be culled from the people involved despite the abuse, and then moves on.

Healthy children are eager to forgive. You have to LEARN how to hold on for an eternity to a resentment. For example, last week my daughter and I were at a birthday party for a little girl. There were a lot of children there, perhaps too many. The place was very crowded, and was buzzing with excitement and sugar-induced energy. There were also a lot of four-letter words there (boys) so the party got a bit rowdy. The parents present got a little concerned, discussed the wildness going on, and decided it was okay for the kids to act like kids at a party. It wasn't realistic to expect them to act like bankers discussing art, or artists discussing money, at an art opening. They let loose and had fun.

But one little girl, in all the excitement, popped the birthday girl in the nose. The mother of the birthday girl became very upset, called the offending child's mother, and told her she would have to come and pick up her daughter. The punishment the hostess decided upon was to not allow the "boxer" to attend the sleep-over to which all the little girls had been invited.

While the mother was on her way over to the birthday party to pick up her daughter, lots of kisses, hugs, and an ice pack were bestowed upon the birthday girl. It is a terrible thing to get slugged in the face on your birthday but, somehow, by the time the mother arrived, the birthday girl and her friends were begging the hostess to allow the "boxer" to stay for the sleep-over. The two mothers discussed this possibility. One mother said that a decision had been reached, and they would have to abide by it, or it would confuse the children. The other mother was embarrassed and defensive about her daughter's behavior. The responses of both mothers were perfectly understandable. The result, however, was that the child had to leave the party.

There is rarely, if ever, a clear "right" and "wrong" side to these situations. "Good guys" and "bad guys" often wear the same colored hat. But that is not the key issue here. What I find most interesting is that both mothers, I happen to know, were raised in dysfunctional homes. Both felt threatened by this "act of violence." Both felt the need to do something in order to fix it. Neither parent looked at how unlikely it is that only one child had caused the episode, and how the birthday girl might have provoked the "boxer." Both mothers failed to take into account that children in their innocence can sometimes be vicious. Both parents were, perhaps, reacting to the pain of similar situations in their own childhoods, which they projected onto their children—and then tried to save them from. It was the parents' responses to the children's issue, more so than the children or the issue, that spoiled the party.

My point in these two stories—the one about my daughter telling me that she didn't blame my parents for the way they raised me, and the other about the scuffle at the birthday party—is that children raised in nurturing homes are willing and eager to forgive. Children, of course, still have their feelings hurt, cry, scream "I hate you," and claim they will never speak to the person again, just as adults sometimes do. But healthy children find it easier to forgive—to let go and move on—because they have love, respect, and acceptance, which are necessary tools for forgiveness.

Healthy children seem to believe that people are basically good. They sense a balance, a stabilizing effect that is built into all conflict. Part of that basic goodness in people is the freedom to get upset, to make a mistake, to feel sorry for doing so, to make amends as best you know how, and then to get back to the party.

Healthy children have a lot of answers to questions they can't even formulate. They instinctively seem to know how to deal with many of their problems. Children left alone will often figure out a solution to their own conflicts. I am sometimes jealous of how simple and complete their conflict resolutions are. I have learned something about negotiating for my own needs by listening to children create and then agree on rules governing their own behavior, without the guidance (or interference) of adults.

It is we adults raised in dysfunctional homes who have to learn that whisking a child out of conflict by taking him or her home to be alone is not necessarily the best way to help the child learn to deal with others. We adults, whom our children sometimes observe as we act like retaliators and blame-seekers, are the carriers of dysfunction from one generation to the next.

We teach what we know. But we can often learn, from children, new ways of dealing with old problems. Forgiveness is a natural function of a healthy spirit. Children can be great teachers. We stand to learn a lot from the deep-seated, open-ended spiral of forgiveness growing ever upward in the spirit of a well-loved, well-nurtured child.

The day after the birthday party where the hitting took place, my daughter and I sat at the breakfast table where we often discuss things from the previous day which we feel were unresolved. I decided I would conduct a little "interview" with her on the subject of forgiveness.

"Let's imagine that it is raining one morning and we are on our way to school. Someone gets on the bus and shakes an umbrella all over your brand-new school clothes and then walks away whistling, like nothing happened. Could you forgive that person?" I asked her.

"Yes," she said adamantly, "because they didn't know they were doing it." My daughter is a little better than I am about presuming the perpetrator innocent until proven guilty. She assumed the person meant no harm. She appears to have a basically positive attitude toward people and life.

"I have another question for you, Celeste." Celeste licked her lips. She savors being included in what sounds like an adult conversation almost as much as she enjoys ice cream. She wiggled around in her seat to get comfortable, the way people do who are being interviewed on Sunday afternoon television quiz shows.

"This is not your usual rainstorm, Celeste," I continued. "Let's imagine it rained all the next day also. The same person got on the bus and shook the umbrella on your clothes again. The person knew it, but kept on walking and didn't say anything. Could you forgive THAT person?"

"No," she snapped, and then paused for a moment and said, "Yes. I mean, maybe." She thought about it a little while longer. "I could forgive them but it would be hard. Maybe I wouldn't want to forgive them. Are you supposed to?"

"It depends," I said, admitting to myself that my answer was a cop-out, but, more importantly, not wanting to take the focus off her feelings as she scanned me for clues to the "right" answer.

"Celeste, this is an unbelievable storm! Three days in a row! We get on the bus and the person who shook their umbrella on your new clothes for the past two days gets on again. Just as the person is about to shake the umbrella again, you shout out, 'Hey! Be careful with the umbrella! You shook that on me for the last two days!' What if that person said, 'So what?' and walked away? Could you forgive the person then?"

"No way," Celeste said defiantly.

"What if the person said, 'I'm sorry'?" I asked.

"I would forgive him," Celeste said with confidence and finality.

I noted with interest, but without drawing a conclusion or asking Celeste about it, that she assigned a masculine gender to the "villain" in the scenario, even though I intentionally didn't assign a "him" or "her" status to the umbrella-shaker.

It seemed that central to my daughter's ability and willingness to forgive is a desire for the person she is trying to forgive to make an apology or to assume at least some responsibility for his or her part in the problem.

All issues in life seem to invoke questions of balance, and a case could be made concerning the person who chronically says "I'm sorry," so that he or she may be forgiven in order to continue to offend again, knowing that forgiveness waits like a hot meal at the end of the day. Chronic or habitual abuse or neglect, coupled with a person's inability or refusal to assume responsibility for the transgression, places the problem in an entirely different arena.

So does the age of the offended. Adults have the option to pull away from or leave an abusive relationship. Children are not always able to drop out of school or run away from home, so they avoid the abuse as best they can. Children often run within.

That is what happened to me as a child. I ran inside. I pulled my isolation over me like a blanket. I snuggled up against the warm fire of my anger. I treated my resentment like a pet—stroking it, talking to it, feeding it. My hurt turned to anger. My willingness to forgive became a difficulty with forgiveness which turned into a refusal to forgive. Brick by brick, I built a fortress around me until it was complete and I felt safe. But I forgot to build a door. No one could get in, which was the way I had planned it. But I couldn't get out, and that was more than I had bargained for. I don't want to live in a fortress. I want to live in a home. Forgiveness is the door leading out of a cold, enclosed heart.

My daughter has an imperfect father. I'm sure I'm committing blunders I don't even recognize that my daughter will grow up and try to forgive me for. I'm doing the best I can, but that is no guarantee that Celeste will not have to work through some unhealthy parenting practices I unknowingly employ. I don't want to cause my precious little daughter any pain, but I know it will happen, to some degree or other.

I don't want to cause myself any unnecessary pain either, but I know that it is my own unresolved issues that I see surfacing in my child that hurt the most. Issues of pain and forgiveness arise between children. They arise between adults. They most certainly arise between children and adults. It happens in all families, not just dysfunctional ones. Children and adults alike are hurt in a gridlock of anger and stubborn unforgiveness.

I have met people who are afraid to have children for fear that, because of the way they were raised, they will ruin their child's life. I have also met many people who are learning how to have intimate relationships despite the way they were raised. These people are learning how to love in a new and better way than the way in which they were once loved. That very love is the sustenance of our future generations. I have hope that, because of the work I am doing, the closest my daughter will ever come to the kind of abuse I knew will be to read a book about it.

The day may come when my daughter will not be able to identify emotionally with some of the relationship issues her father has. To an extent, this has already happened. Fear of intimacy, shame, terminal shyness, stuffed feelings—these are absent in her character. I have seen my eight-year-old daughter scratch her head in loving puzzlement about what life must be like with so much fear. I am sometimes almost embarrassed at not being as healthy as she is in some areas of my life. She is a different person than I am. She doesn't have to run away from home. She doesn't have to hide within herself. She can't relate to being raised in a dysfunctional home. Amazing!

There is an expression: "What goes around comes around." I interpret it to mean that as I learn, sometimes from my daughter, to be more forgiving of others, I learn to be more forgiving of myself. I learn to forgive myself, for example, for not being a perfect parent. I allow myself to make mistakes. Then I begin to allow my daughter to make mistakes also. As my daughter begins to see me learn to be a forgiving person who can let go of, instead of clinging to, a resentment, she sees the possibility and benefits of forgiveness.

I define forgiveness as letting go, lightening up, and moving on to more fruitful things—like love. We need not pass on to future generations what was passed on to us. A cold heart is hereditary. Love, acceptance, and forgiveness are contagious. I am a perfectly imperfect parent with a perfectly imperfect child, with whom I have a perfectly imperfect relationship. Wanting it any other way would be utterly unforgivable.

Yikes! The Dentist!

Celeste blamed herself when we found out that she had a lot of dental work to be done. She cried and said that she wished she had never eaten any candy in her whole life. She pushed her fist hard into her leg as she was saying that, as if she were trying to punish herself.

I explained to her that candy had a lot to do with it, but that poor dental habits were also a part of the reason. Then I tried to explain to her that being prone to cavities was hereditary.

"What's hereditary?" she wanted to know.

I tried to explain and, after grappling with the concept for a few minutes, Celeste did an about-face and began to blame ME for her cavities. I had cavities as a kid. I passed it along to her somehow through my "jeans." It was suddenly all my fault!

Celeste had shifted the blame from herself to me. I couldn't deal with the waves of guilt that washed over me as I viewed myself as the cause of the dental agony Celeste was going to experience over the next two months. So I did the natural thing.

I shifted the blame from me to . . . television commercials! I took a deep breath and said, "You know those television commercials that tell you to go out and buy those lousy, junky, sugary, crappy, yucko cereals?" I was exaggerating my emotions as well as my gestures.

"Yeah," Celeste said simply and with eager attention, sensing another of her father's monologues coming on.

"Well, those commercials are made by grown-ups who know very well what sugar does to the teeth of children," I said, as if a sinister plot against children had been revealed (and it had). "And this," I said, "is what I would like to do to them." I smashed the fist of one hand into the open palm of the other. I made a loud, cracking noise. "I'd like to kaboink them right in the nose for what they're doing to precious little children like you."

The blame was off her. The blame was off me. We stood united against pain and plaque and sugar-pushers!

But we were still sitting in a dentist's office on a late winter Thursday afternoon when the sun set at 4:30. Celeste was seven years old. The world of Sugar Plum Fairies and Gingerbread Houses came crashing down upon her. An era had ended. Suddenly we found ourselves living in a new era of responsibility, control, and prevention. What a shame that I had to tell my daughter how the fun you have today may come back to haunt you tomorrow. I know that lesson is important and inevitable, but it certainly is too bad you can't get away with certain things at least until tomorrow.

And speaking of tomorrow, how do I explain to Celeste that I just retrieved a message on my answering machine from the director of our church school, asking that we bring a bag of jelly beans to church on Sunday because the kids will be assembling bags of "goodies" for the children who have to be in the hospital over the Easter holiday? Doesn't that make us just like the people who make those candy commercials for television?

I hate to be the bearer of truth.

Celeste woke up the day after her first visit to the dentist and she began to cry. She didn't even want to sit up, let alone go to school and let the kids see her silver tooth. She wanted to lie in bed and feel sorry for herself. I allowed her to do just that, for a while. I was tempted to interrupt her self-pity by telling her how I was a cripple for five years as a kid, and I had to give up a lot more than candy. I had to give up walking. I could have told her how my marvelous smile had cost me a fortune, because my parents didn't care enough to take me to the dentist when I was a child. I also might have told her how I had to give up drinking alcohol years ago and how hard it was to do it, and how I missed it for a long time, and how I felt that it was unfair that other people got to drink and I didn't. I was tempted to tell her how sugar is not only bad for your teeth, but that it is bad for your entire body.

But I didn't. I just kept my mouth shut and allowed her to have her own feelings without judgment, interference, or comparison with my feelings. It is so hard to just sit and watch my child have painful or uncomfortable feelings. The temptation is great to jump in and try to save her from life. Instead of telling her all the bad things, I suddenly wanted to bombard her with greatness and gratitude! I wanted to tell her how all my sacrifices had been worth it, how this isn't so bad and that isn't so bad, how pain is such a great teacher. I wanted to say, "Think of all the starving children in China," but I didn't.

Children are resilient. They can spring back from almost any trauma, if they know they are loved. They don't need to be told that everything is okay, because some things aren't okay. Some things are a real drag.

Like no candy.

Celeste already, one day after the bad news that she can never have candy again except on her birthday, is coming to terms with the new sugarless era of her life. She actually kind of likes the extra attention, and the ritual of flossing and brushing with special gels.

She doesn't understand, but I know what will follow. There will be bright lights and strange smells and shots and the drill. I don't want to save my daughter from reality. I don't want to show her the escape route that I traveled for my entire life until I was thirty. I just want to be there for her when the pain and fear seem larger than life itself. I want to be there so that she might find herself GROWING through pain rather than GOING through it.

I hope my love is enough, for a starter, because it seems like all I have, at the moment, to offer. I'm ready to face the challenge.

Money Where Your Mouth Is

It was quite a challenge to face. The dentist was the best specialist in children's dentistry I could find in New York. The first visit, at full office visit cost, was the dentist holding Celeste's hand and giving her a tour of the office, a ride up and down in the dental chair, and the two of them counting teeth together.

The second and all subsequent visits were the real stuff. Celeste's initial pride about being such a good girl quickly faded into dread of yet another appointment. Several days before and several days after each appointment were marred by expectation of and recovery from the visits. That meant that virtually every day of the week was tainted by the dentist.

Celeste was upset, and I didn't blame her. I remember feeling the same way when I was a kid. The nicer the dentist was, the more confused I became. If the dentist is so nice, why is she hurting me?

The other day when Celeste was in dire dread of the next visit, I said to her, "You know, Celeste, when I was a little boy my parents didn't take very good care of me. They let my teeth get very bad and they didn't fix them. When I grew up I was still so mad at them that I wrote a chapter in one of my books about it. I'm now wondering, Celeste, if you are mad at me?"

"I'm mad at everybody, including me," she said.

"Why you?" I asked.

"Because I ate the candy."

"But I gave you the candy."

There was a long pause as Celeste sat silently for a sullen moment.

"Why DID you give me all that candy, Daddy?"

I began to sob a little. Celeste was fascinated with my tears. She had tapped the immense puddle of guilt that lies dormant in me, and now it was flooding my soul. Sometimes I am overcome with great fear, unsubstantiated by any word or deed, that I am going to ruin my daughter's life. It is a fear that because of the way I was raised, I will never be able to raise a child properly, no matter how hard I try or how good my intentions. I am usually quite good at dispelling that myth, but sometimes, at a weak moment like this, I succumb to it.

"I knew you had tooth problems," I said to her, "but I let you have candy anyway. I just hoped the problem would go away. I wanted you to be able to have candy like the other kids and I hated to have to say no to you. So now you have a lot of cavities. Please don't be mad at yourself. You're just a little girl and you couldn't have known that this dentist stuff would be the result of eating sugar. But I knew. So I wouldn't blame you a bit if you were mad at me, because I'm mad at me for letting you have that stuff. You have a right to be mad at me. But I want you to know that I didn't hurt you on purpose. I try to do my best and I can't do everything right. I goofed up. But I am doing everything I can to help you now. We're going to get through this. We're already off sugar. The dental work will be done in a few weeks. Then we will be able to make sure that it never gets this bad again. The worst is over. Let's try to be brave and get rid of this problem once and for all."

Celeste lightened up. I knew she felt better. I can guess at a few reasons why. For one thing, I validated her feelings. It was obvious to me that she was angry about having to have the work done. It was also obvious that she wasn't expressing that anger directly. I encouraged her to be angry at even her own father, because anger was there, and it was appropriate. I let her know that I was not angry at her for being angry at me and her mother.

She saw me taking responsibility for my part in her problem. I showed her that, in addition to being her father, I am also a struggling person who is not always right. I allowed her to see a grown man cry over something he has and has not done, as well as how the accepting of these uncomfortable feelings eased my sadness and anger. I tried to pry my feelings out of that guilt, so that I could see them more clearly and discuss them. She saw me doing everything I could to correct the problem I had, in part, caused. She saw me trying to help her, as well as loving and accompanying her on her painful journey.

Celeste is learning that pain is not a word without end. She is learning that pain is an episode, not a way of life. She is gaining insight and strength through this dental experience because of her own courage and faith and because of my guidance.

Six months have passed since Celeste finished her dental work. She has taken incredibly good care of her teeth. We went for a check-up and she had no cavities. That's not bad for a kid who can get cavities from eating a hamburger. Before she got out of the dental chair, I handed her a camera I bought for her as a celebration of her good work. I took a picture of her, the dentist, and the hygienist.

Celeste walked out of that office feeling like a hero. I told her that I am very proud of her and, most importantly, I hoped she was very proud of herself, because she is the one who did it. For the first time, Celeste was able to see that her efforts and determination had created change in her life. I could see the new sensation of courage, confidence, and power reflected in her eyes. I am a good father with a wonderful child. It sure feels good to be able to say that.

Is Santa Dead?

"Celeste found out there isn't a Santa," her mother said to me.

"How did she find out?"

"I told her."

"Why did you tell her?"

"Because she asked, and I didn't want to lie."

"How did she take it?" I asked.

"Not well."

"What does that mean?"

"She cried for two hours."

"Then she wasn't ready to hear it," I said.

"That's right, Dwight, she wasn't ready to hear it," my former wife snapped.

"Then what happened?" I asked.

"She went into her room and came out with a small gift in her hands that she had made for Santa and she asked me, 'Now what do I do with this?'"

Ouch! Hearing that really hurt. I absorbed the pain in silence and then asked, "What did you do then?"

"I just had to laugh," my former wife said.

"You laughed?"

"Yes," she said, "The situation was just so ironic. It just became absurd, so I laughed."

Celeste was already in bed at her mother's house. There was nothing I could say or do that night. I would see Celeste the next day.

"Oh, well," I sadly slurred, "Oh, well."

"I didn't want to lie to her," my wife repeated.

"I don't understand," I said, "what lies and truth have to do with the existence of Santa Claus."

We ended the conversation.

I went to bed and wondered, What is our hurry to yank our child out of her state of innocence? I believe that Santa does indeed exist, but we adults talk ourselves out of the ability to see him. Prove to me that I am wrong! I believe there is a world of the spiritual that coexists, like concentric circles, with the world of the material. To "see" the spiritual world, all we have to do is to be willing to believe that it exists. We need not believe. We need only to be willing to believe. The spiritual world is present today just as much as it was in the day of Shakespeare. They had no problem with ghosts walking out on stage. They had more acceptance of the spiritual world, not because they were stupid or superstitious, but because they were more willing to see.

The choice, it seems to me, is between allowing a child a dream or stepping on that dream. Is it a lie to extend hope to someone who is very ill? Should we outlaw all songs that refer to the Man in the Moon because now we know better? Is it a lie when a mime artist sits down on a chair that isn't there? Shakespeare wrote a play called *Hamlet* in which three ghosts walk out on stage. No one stood up in the audience and yelled "liar" to the actors. The audience simply suspended their disbelief until the need to believe in the unlikely was over.

We literal-minded, modern adults do not fully understand the function of a child's communication with spirits. We indulge our very young children a little bit, as when a child sits and has a lengthy conversation with a refrigerator. We don't stop children from doing this in the name of "truth," do we? Then why do we stop them when they grow older?

There is an unintentional conspiracy on the part of adults to narrow the spiritual horizons of children down to a size that is not threatening to us. We do it in the name of preparing them for adulthood. We also do it out of fear that if we allow our children to believe in and communicate with spirits we cannot see, then we will lose control of our children, and they will fall under the influence of "evil spirits" who will drive them to Bellevue.

I happen to know that Santa Claus was my daughter's guardian angel. And now I know that she won't let him come and visit her anymore. Guardian angels are very obedient.

When you don't need or want them anymore, they leave. Children intuitively know when they no longer need the guidance and protection of their guardian angels. It is at that point that children are ready to move on and assume some of the responsibility of loving and guiding and protecting themselves.

A child who gently and silently releases her or his guardian angel is much different from a child asking, "Is there a Santa Claus?" A child asking such a question is not pleading for an intellectual discussion of lies and truth. The child is asking for the parent to validate the existence of the strong rush of feelings and spirit-force which, for want of a better word, we might as well call "Santa," but which others might call "God" and still others might call "soul." Giving a child a dream and then snatching it away is cruelty. Allowing a child to release the spirit of Santa, so he can go to other children in need of his grace, is an act of love.

There is another aspect of my daughter's conclusion that "there isn't a Santa Claus." It is the severity of my response. The anger I felt at my former wife was incredible! Her handling of the "Santa Affair" was at worst a mistake. But I reacted as if she had ruined Celeste's life.

Through my daughter, I felt for the first time the pain I had known as a kid when I found out that there wasn't a Santa. I was stunned. As a kid being raised in a crazy family, I needed my guardian angel a lot longer than a lot of kids do. Without my guardian angel I would not have survived. I didn't know how to deal with the fact that doubt had been placed between me and my first God, whom I chose to call Santa. And the doubt had been placed there by my very own parents. Out of loyalty to them, I abandoned my belief. That was the day I wordlessly asked my guardian angel to leave.

Numbness overcame me and I never thought about Santa again until Celeste was going through the same thing. My daughter was the catalyst through which I felt the feelings that were never felt the first time around. And they hurt. I felt lied to. Betrayed. Stunned. My world had been wounded and all the magic was running out of it. I felt pale. And numb. And silly for having believed in the first place.

And I didn't feel like a child anymore. Yeah. That's it. My only connection to the childhood I never had was to be aware of the child who still dwells within me. And my daughter has gone through a passageway. The loss of the belief in Santa is a rite of passage out of young childhood. My daughter has gone through that passageway. She is not a baby anymore. And neither am I.

I tried to stuff the magic back into the myth. I listened to the wise counsel of friends and other parents. I talked at length with Celeste about the spirit of Christmas and love and giving and peace. I asked her if she had any questions.

"Yeah," she said. "Who put the presents under the tree?"

"I did."

"No more questions," she said as she turned on the television.

Santa is now molded chocolate with a chocolate beard and chocolate boots all wrapped in brightly colored foil. Santa is now kids' stuff.

So the inevitable has happened. Celeste has been told that there is no Santa and she believes it. I don't think she was ready for it. But like any other of her life experiences, I see my job as being supportive of her no matter what my opinion of it is.

I want to make sure that just because Santa is gone from her life, that doesn't mean that the magic and miracles of life have to be gone also.

Santa is dead. Long live Santa!

Christmas with and without Andrea

I can't deal with Christmas very well. Single parent. Memories of my childhood Christmas tree untrimmed and leaning in a corner. A seemingly insignificant birthday hidden between Christmas and New Year's Eve. Yuck!

Last year I decided to take Celeste to the Bahamas for the holiday, or at least the better part of it. We arrived back in New York City late in the night on Christmas Eve. We went straight from the airport to a party. It seemed a little like Christmas, but not much. Wet, sandy beach towels gave off a salty odor from within my canvas suitcase. My sunburn was killing me. My daughter was tired, so we couldn't stay long. Yes. My plan had worked. I didn't feel a bit of the Christmas spirit.

Andrea was at the party and asked if she could come home with me and my daughter. I paused. Christmas Eve. She is alone in a foreign country. Yes. She could come home with us. I pulled my daughter aside and told her that Andrea would come home with us so that Andrea and I could talk after she went to bed. That was fine with my daughter.

Celeste immediately fell asleep. Andrea and I chatted a little while and then we went to bed and made love. We fell into a contented sleep. I woke in the middle of the night and went to the bathroom. I looked over at the towel rack and saw Andrea's panties and bra flung over it. I was stunned! What if Celeste had gotten up in the middle of the night to go to the bathroom and saw the panties and bra there? Celeste didn't even know Andrea was still there. No woman had ever spent the night with me when Celeste was there. A matching set of black silk panties and bra would be her introduction to a woman being somewhere in the house. I didn't like that. As a matter of fact, it really bothered me. I couldn't believe Andrea could be so casual as to leave her clothes lying around for Celeste to discover. It seemed very insensitive to me.

I became concerned that Andrea had no emotional boundaries. I got into a paranoid state of mind and said to myself, This woman moves right into my space! She must be stopped! I must create distance from her. Damn! I should have told Celeste that Andrea was going to spend the night! What was I thinking of to allow my daughter to wake up and see this naked Belgian climbing out of my loft bed on Christmas morning? I should have known better. Why would I do something like that?

It was 3:30 in the morning. I was standing naked in the dark kitchen of my apartment. Tenderness, a sense of companionship and family, love, confusion, and panic were settling into my Christmas soul. I felt I had to hide her clothes! I felt I had to hide her body! I took the bra and panties off the towel rack and held them under my arm. I walked toward the bedroom and collected her other clothes on my way. I struggled up the ladder leading to my loft bed carrying her sweater, socks, pants, and scarf. Andrea woke up and watched me lay all of her clothes at the foot of the bed. I crawled under the sheets, laid on my back, put my hands behind my head, and stared at the ceiling.

"Why didn't you bring up my boots and coat too?" a soft, European voice asked in the darkness. There was a thick, thick aura of silence and isolation around me. I was like a block of ice that radiates cold to whoever's hand is close to it, even without touching it.

"This isn't fair to Celeste," I said. "I should have talked to her about it first." We both lay still in the darkness.

"Should I go?"

"No," I said, "but I want to leave this bed and go sleep on the couch. Then she will think you just spent the night, like a friend from out of town. I'll tell her it was too late for you to go home, so I invited you to stay."

"Whatever you wish."

I climbed down out of my bed. I thought I had made the right decision. I also thought about Andrea lying awake in my bed, alone, on Christmas Eve, thinking about how screwed-up this situation was. I felt torn, like an old sheet being converted into little rags. I had a throbbing head and felt nauseous. I wanted to call my therapist, my spiritual advisor, my minister, or even my dermatologist! I wanted to call ANYBODY who could tell me what to do!

But it was 3:30 in the morning. Celeste was sound asleep, possibly dreaming of a trampoline she mastered in the Bahamas. Or of the presents that awaited her, delivered for the first time by someone other than the Santa she had recently decided not to believe in. It was 3:30 in the morning and I was torn between a woman and a child, between being a boyfriend and being a father. I decided the best thing to do was to close my eyes. I fought my way into a deep, tormented, buzzing, dreamless, drug-like stupor of a sleep.

Celeste woke me up a few hours later. "I thought you were Andrea," she said to me. We all got up and opened presents. Andrea was wearing my bathrobe. Celeste had no problem with that, or with her being there. I was the one who had the problem. I got the distinct impression that Celeste could have cared less if Andrea and I slept together or not. As a matter of fact, I think it would have seemed a little more normal to her if we had.

A little while later Andrea went home and I took Celeste to her mother's house where she would spend the rest of Christmas Day. All I could do was to hope that I had done the right thing. I hoped Andrea wasn't too upset with me, and I hoped I would learn not to be so upset with myself.

I'll Blow Your House Down

It's nice to get your feelings out into the open where they belong, but that doesn't mean that healing will automatically take place because you decided to get honest. My former wife and I, for example, had been at great odds about Celeste's schooling and several other issues for a long time. A lot of painful things were discussed at length. A lot of repressed, ill feelings were brought to the surface. A lot of things were resolved. But I was still left with a horrible feeling because I knew that, despite getting the feelings out into the open, too much pain had been left unmentioned for too long for much healing to take place.

I'm lucky. After an argument with my former wife, I get to walk away. Her future husband, however, is the one who has to deal with the aftereffects of our arguments. Perhaps that is why, the morning after one of my arguments with my former wife, when I called and asked to speak with my daughter, my daughter's future stepfather, Bob, answered the phone and said:

"Dwight, call back later," and then he hung up on me.

There is a saying that when you become enraged you "see red." Well, it's true! Red came racing in from the periphery of my vision, like a gallon of red paint spilled on a white, linoleum floor. I called Bob back. My former wife answered the phone.

"He can't come to the phone right now," she said.

I repeated that I wanted to speak with Bob. She repeated that I couldn't. First he stood between me and my daughter, and then my former wife stood between me and him.

"Let me talk to him!" I demanded.

She hung up the phone. I called back. The phone had been taken off the hook. I gave up trying. Twenty minutes later my daughter called me. She had just woken up, she informed me, and had been told that I had called. She had been asleep all the while I was fighting for the right to talk to her! Why didn't they simply tell me that?

Celeste and I talked about her loose tooth and a few things, but I couldn't keep my concentration.

"Let me talk to Bob," I said to Celeste.

She tried to get him to come to the phone, but he wouldn't. My former wife, once again, came to the phone to speak on his behalf and then, once again, hung up on me. Once again I called her back and said:

"I'm coming over."

It was my turn to hang up.

You may be wondering why I got so upset in the first place. As a child I was a quiet, polite, little crippled boy. I had a leg disease that prohibited me from walking until I was seven years old. I sat in a corner of my room, reading, for virtually all of my childhood. No one worried about me. They didn't have to. I was perfect. The belief of my family was that I was a very strong, centered, rational child who could take anything. I was destined to be a famous lawyer, they told each other countless times. That was their excuse, I guess, for leaving me in the corner, unattended, while they dealt with the constant, daily lunacy of the other members of the family.

And what was going on inside me? I was a cripple both inside and out. I was so terrified I couldn't move. I felt as if I were rotting. I felt invisible, taken for granted, that my needs were not taken into consideration. I felt passed-over and unnoticed. And, lo and behold, while still a very young man, I collapsed into alcoholism. And then, while still quite young, I began my recovery, and vowed never again to let people take me for granted. And I vowed never again to punish myself for letting people do it.

So when my former wife and her fiancé hung up on me, it was the final blow to my self-esteem that I could tolerate from them. I could understand that they were trying to build a new life on their own. I was struggling to come to terms with my envy of their relationship—not necessarily the quality of it—but the mere existence of it. I had come to accept that Bob was living in what I considered to be my house, and sleeping on the bed that I had built. I could understand that Bob had to set up some rules between himself and my daughter.

When Bob refused to let me talk to my daughter, who is the only person in the world I feel connected to, I felt left out and left behind for the last time!

I called from a phone booth on a corner of their block. My former wife answered the phone.

"I'm in the phone booth outside your apartment, standing in the rain, waiting for Bob to come down. I want to talk to him for three minutes."

"He's very busy and can't come out."

Click. She hung up again.

My former wife just didn't understand! I didn't want to hit him. I only wished to talk to him! I wanted to tell him that I knew I was out of control, that I was scared and in pain. I wanted to tell him that there was nothing in life I feared more than losing the love of my daughter. I wanted him to know that I had been practicing calling him her "stepfather" so that when he and my former wife got married, I would be ready for the presence of a new father figure in my daughter's life. But he wouldn't come to the damn phone—or come down to meet with me!

Finally, after unsuccessfully storming their apartment in a vain attempt to see him, I went to work and called him from there. Celeste, who had been caught in the middle of all this, had calmed down after having a long talk with her mother and him, he told me. I suggested that he and I should get together and talk. He said he would, if there was a third party present. I asked him if he was concerned that I was going to bop him in the nose.

That was not his concern, he assured me. He just couldn't deal with aggression in any form. He told me that one reason why he was gruff on the phone with me is that every time I talk to my former wife he has to pick her up off the floor with a spoon. I hurt her a lot, he said. That was revealing to me. I had always thought that her only response to me was numbness. I often found myself trying to break through her numbness, as if I had to chisel her out of ice before I could talk to her. He also said that I never say hello or good morning to him. I'm never nice. I just bark something into the phone like, "Let me talk to my daughter." He was right, although I wasn't prepared to tell him so. I did tell him that I would call him later in the week and try to set up an appointment to meet with him. He agreed.

I picked up Celeste from school that afternoon and she immediately wanted to talk about who was right and who was wrong.

"The entire situation is very unfortunate," I said to her, "and there is no clear right and wrong side."

Now the true grief was beginning to set in. And the guilt. I was becoming immersed in it. I began to see the damage that had been inflicted on my daughter, and I couldn't believe what I had done. I am usually so controlled and eloquent. I usually wait until Celeste is asleep before I have an intense conversation with her mother.

What did that incident say, I wondered, about my willingness to sacrifice Celeste to the fires of my need to be right and in control? Was I really willing to let Celeste get caught in the crossfire between me and the man who would be her stepfather? Why was my pride more important than my daughter? Was it true that I simply couldn't stop myself when the feelings became that strong? What did that say of my ability, after five years of separation, to let go of my former wife?

I was still dragging my former wife along behind me like a little red wagon filled with resentment. She was still a gauze-wrapped icon that I worshipped. I was still doing a tightrope walk above her head, while she was busy taking down the safety net as quickly as possible. And I thought I was unaffected by her impending marriage! A lot of this fight seemed to be about me trying to maintain dominion in the Unholy Trinity of me, my former wife, and her fiancé. No wonder I lashed out at her and Bob. But I was the carrier of most of the anger. And I was the one who suffered the most because of it.

And what of my daughter? Celeste seemed split right down the middle, having to choose between love on the one hand, and love on the other. She seemed torn in two. No matter which way she turned, she would be turning her back on one of her parents. I wondered just how much damage had been done—if this would be one of the torrid events that her memory would dangle in front of her when she grew older and contemplated marriage. I wondered if she would ever forgive me, if she would ever heal.

I also wondered if I would ever forgive myself, if I would ever heal. Would I ever be in a relationship again, or had my attitudes toward women been so badly damaged that I could never trust again? I understood, a bit, why I had acted the way I had. I had compassion for myself. But I also was sad, disappointed, and angry at myself.

I asked Celeste if she was mad at me. She said she wanted to speak to Sheila, the school psychologist. I felt good about my daughter, who is only seven years old, being able to ask for help. But it was also kind of sad. Here was a seven-year-old girl from a broken home asking for professional help. I told her that, if she was mad at me, it was okay because I was a grown-up and could take it. I talked to her, as her mother and I have done for her entire life, about the importance of getting her feelings out, no matter what the feelings were. She is and always has been very emotionally expressive.

The next morning Celeste was okay, not great, but okay. She and I both seemed to have an emotional hangover from the madness of the day before. She was still insistent on choosing sides. At that moment, I was more right than her mother was. I told her to prepare herself for me seeming more right in our house, and her mother seeming more right in hers. I also reminded her that it was the situation that was bad, not the people in it. I explained that situations can go very wrong sometimes, but that people can learn to solve their problems. I told her that Mommy and Daddy arguing would never result in us not loving our child. I also said it was possible that everyone could end up getting along better as a result of the fight. But underneath all that smooth, positive talk, I was terrified that I was inflicting on my daughter the same thing that was inflicted on me as a child. Abuse.

As a kid, there was a fight in my home every day for the seventeen years that I lived with my parents. There was never a hint of a resolution. Each argument was added to the mass of former arguments like flour being kneaded into a bread dough. Nothing ever got better. My wounds never healed, as the scabs were torn off every night by yet another claw taking a swipe at my attempts to heal, until I finally gave up trying to recover, and wrapped my wounds in layer after layer of numbness.

Two days passed until I saw Celeste again. In that period of time, I did several things to try to help us:

1. I called Celeste's teacher immediately on the morning of the incident and told her of the fight Celeste's mother and I had that Celeste was caught in. I asked the teacher to be especially understanding of Celeste if she showed signs of difficulty with concentration, or fatigue, or whatever.

2. I called the school psychologist and told her what had happened. I told her that Celeste had requested a visit with her. The psychologist saw Celeste alone. Then I met with the psychologist, as did her mother, on a separate occasion. It was unfortunate that her mother and I were still too upset to meet with the psychologist together.

3. I called Bob in the early evening on the day after the "incident." I knew he wasn't home, but I didn't want to call when Celeste was awake. I left a message on the answering machine saying that I wanted to meet with him for ten minutes or so. I told him it could be at any time on any day. We could meet in the park, a restaurant, or anywhere that he liked.

   When I got home later that night, there was a message on my machine from my former wife. She said that Bob was very busy for the entire weekend, and could not meet with me. I was not happy. There she was speaking for him again. Being as generous as I could be, I told myself that it was none of my business which of them called me and left a message on my machine. I told myself that Bob had a right to be tired, or scared, or not ready to face me yet. I was sure that both of them were very hesitant to trust me after my rampage. I reminded myself that just because I was ready and eager to change doesn't mean that someone else will be ready to do the same.

4. I went and talked to my minister about the incident for an hour and a half. He suggested that I "eat some crow" and admit that I was wrong to go over there. He suggested that, as the wedding approached, I might try to let go of Celeste a little bit, and be careful that we not cling to each other. He said their wedding was bound to have an impact on both of us. He made a strong case for patience and time, and for my learning to be less obsessive.

5. I spent a long Saturday night sitting home, alone, in my pajamas, with a pot pie in the oven, thinking about what went wrong. I knew the answer was not to punish myself for being an imperfect parent. I also knew that enough is enough. I wanted to learn new ways of dealing with old problems.

A few weeks passed. Silence and time bandaged the wounds between my former wife and me enough so we could speak about what had happened. She told me that Celeste tried very hard, out of loyalty to me, to not love Bob. She said my daughter thinks she has to love either me or him. She loves me very much, so she tries to kill her love for him. That hurt. I had spent a lifetime trying to withhold love from people as a way of punishing them. It didn't help. I hurt myself very badly doing that.

I came to realize that the incident was a turning point in my life. I began, one day at a time, to reach out to Bob, to accept him as my former wife's new husband. I was not particularly fond of him, but Celeste saw me being consistently kind and polite to him. I was acting, I will admit. But eventually I realized he wasn't such a bad person. He told me that he thought Celeste had two good parents, and he saw no need for him to step in and provide for Celeste what she already had. I came to believe that, just in case something happened to me, Celeste would be fortunate enough to still have a father figure in her life. When there were school functions, we all sat together. I began to say complimentary things about Bob to Celeste. She began to feel safe in talking to me about problems she was having with him. And by the time the marriage came around, Celeste was able to go to Greece, where it took place, with an open, loving heart. She was able to endorse her mother's marriage. The love in her was flowing out in all directions.

Several months have passed since the wedding. Celeste's mother and I still disagree from time to time on various subjects. Sometimes we get angry with each other. Celeste still gets scared once in a while if she senses that something is up. But I remind her that people—including Celeste and me—do get mad at each other once in a while. That doesn't mean that things have to get nasty.

Her mother and I afford each other a mutual respect. We do not call each other names or begin each argument with blame-tossing. We do not dredge up the past. We view our problems with Celeste as joint ventures aimed toward resolution. Actions, indeed, speak louder than words, and our reasonable communication has not gone unnoticed by Celeste. She is the greatest beneficiary of our improved relationship.

The key has been consistency. I used to sit around waiting for all the ill feelings to go away by themselves. Then I realized that it would take the daily application of love, respect, surrender of control, minding my own business, and prayer for the well-being of those I have problems with to turn a relationship around. In other words, it takes work.

I let go of my attempts to control my former wife and, to a lesser extent, I let go of my daughter as well. The result is that my love for them is changing, growing deeper, more mature. My feeling for them has an eternal quality that I find very hard to explain. Let me try by saying that it is a love not based on what they do or claim to do. There is no target or scoreboard in my love for them. I need no ticket, approval, or permission to love them. I am not seeking a reward for loving them. And because of this, somehow, I have granted myself permission to be loved by others.

The Mugging

Don't tell me, "That's what you get for living in New York." That is a cold, nasty thing to say. Besides, I have said it to myself a thousand times, and so has everybody else who lives here. Just let me tell my story and then try, without judgment, to understand how I'm feeling.

    I picked up Celeste at school. We went and had dinner. We took the bus home. We got off the bus. I was holding my daughter's hand, as well as two bags of groceries. At the end of the block I glanced across the street and saw three very suspicious-looking young men standing on the corner. I can smell trouble, probably because of the way I was brought up. My senses are finely tuned to detect impending violence. Rather than cross the street, we turned right and began to walk quickly down the block. I glanced over my shoulder to see one of the three men reach into his coat and pull out a gun.

    I looked slightly up the road and saw a family about to enter their apartment building. I literally pulled Celeste down the street as we went up to them and I said, "My daughter and I live across the street. We're about to be mugged by three men. Can we please come into the building with you?" The man invited us in. We stood in the hallway for a moment. I introduced myself and Celeste, who looked pale and too confused to be frightened.

    I asked if we could stay in the hallway for a few minutes. The father called his teenage son out into the hallway. We looked out the window of the hallway door onto the street. One of the muggers was back on the corner, watching the building, as if to see whether Celeste and I would emerge undefended once again.

    We waited until he disappeared around the corner. And then the father and his son offered to walk Celeste and me across the street and safely into our building, which is what they did. I will never forget the loving generosity of that family. The father risked his own and his son's safety in order to provide safety for me and my daughter. And I also will never forget that asking for help probably had saved our lives.

We were safe in our apartment. After we settled down a bit, Celeste asked if we could have been killed. I told her that yes, we could have been killed. She wanted to know what a mugging would have been like. I told her that they would probably take my watch and wallet, as well as her backpack. She could not quite conceive of a mugging, and envisioned it as being replete with "please" and "thank you," as in: "May I please have your wallet now. Thank You."

An hour or so later I put Celeste to bed and sat up thinking. I said a prayer of gratitude that Celeste and I had not been hurt. Having expressed gratitude, I went immediately into a tailspin of rage.

I must tell you that I have been mugged at gunpoint before. It took me a long time to get over it. But this was different because I had a child with me. I guess we all have some sort of denial that reinforces our myth of immortality. My denial was that if I were ever a mugging victim, I would never be killed because I would utter the following words: "I have a kid and no wife. If you kill me, my daughter will be all by herself."

My denial has been shattered. I now know that I was not a potential mugging victim IN SPITE OF being with a child. I was a great mugging prospect BECAUSE I was with a child. I was a man in a nice coat carrying two bags of groceries and holding a child by the hand. I was off balance. I was preoccupied. Those muggers didn't distinguish between a bag of groceries and a child. My daughter's life meant no more to them than a can of tomatoes. I was apparently dealing with people who had no soul, who would not respond to logic or rationality, who could kill a child if she started to cry.

This event inflicted damage on me that is separate but related to the damage caused to my sense of trust and security. For one thing, some life experiences confirm the negative messages that parents or other authority figures gave to you during your childhood. After that almost-mugging, I slid quickly back into my old beliefs that the world is an unsafe place populated by people who can't be trusted.

I work very hard at being a positive, hopeful person, especially because a positive state of mind doesn't come easy for me. Many people are basically positive, but I must admit that I am not one of them. I don't watch television. I don't go to movies that depict senseless violence or exploit women. I protect my newfound vulnerability and fragile sense of trust and love because I know how quick I am to be hurt and disappointed. I don't want to walk around feeling like a potential victim, waiting for a disaster to happen. That is what life was like as a kid and I am trying hard to change that.

I am afraid I will be slow to rebound from this incident. The child within me has gone back into hiding. It will be difficult to convince my inner child that it is safe to come back out into the world. And that upsets me very much.

Another manifestation of the damage done to my soul by the near-miss mugging is that I find myself trying to figure out what I did wrong in order to bring the violence down upon me. One of the things that sickens me about this new age in which we live is the belief that we cause ALL the harm that comes to us. If you have breast cancer, it is because you dislike being a woman. If you have cancer of the colon, it is because you have always been a pain in the ass. If you get mugged, it is because you are walking around with an aura of violence and anger which attracts violence and anger. Perhaps there are elements of truth to these suppositions, but I also believe that stuff simply happens.

The day after the attempted mugging, I went into a spiritual bookstore and two men listened to my story. Almost simultaneously, like Siamese twins connected at the imagination, they essentially asked why I wanted my daughter and me to get mugged. I almost hit them. I chose instead to leave. I don't need some tinhorn guru who "got spiritual" a year ago to try to hold me responsible not only for the pain of the attempted mugging, but also the pain of having forced some poor, young killers to attack me and my precious child.

In the meantime, now that I have gotten some of the ugly, angry feelings of pain and betrayal out of me, I feel a lot better. My daughter had a nightmare the night of our near-miss, in which a woman was beaten to death with a pipe but I, her father, was able to get my daughter away from the danger unharmed. I am so sorry Celeste had to have that dream, but I had expected and was prepared for some reaction to our fearful episode. I could tell by the dream that my daughter feels protected. And she should feel that way. My daughter saw her father do everything within his power to save her. I'm glad she got to see that. All her life she has been told that I am here to love her forever. She has seen that my actions match my words.

I also feel pretty good today about being a seeker in recovery. If it had not been for the hell in which I was raised as a child, and the abuse I suffered at my own hands as an adult, I would not have been able to "smell" trouble. I might not have been able to think so quickly on my feet. I might not have been able to calculate that I had about thirty seconds in which to defend myself before I had to surrender to the inevitable.

I was able to act quickly, appropriately, and courageously on my own behalf. Perhaps being raised in a dysfunctional home saved our lives.

Woman without Child

I had a feeling she didn't like kids, and that is probably why I took so long introducing her to mine. My worst suspicions were confirmed when she and my daughter finally met. Nothing bad happened. But nothing good happened either. When we walked down the street, it was like any other day. But that day was not like any other day in that my daughter was with us. My friend didn't acknowledge my daughter. She just kept talking about herself and looking at me. Naturally, my daughter noticed she wasn't noticed.

When we got to the playground, Celeste ran to the swing. I took a seat on the edge of the sandbox, so I could talk to my friend and keep an eye on my daughter at the same time. My friend took a seat on the edge of the sandbox also, but she positioned herself so that she was facing me, with her back to my daughter.

No thank you, I said to myself. This will never do. A million faceless voices echoed in my ear, saying things like "It's not a bad thing that a woman doesn't like children" and "It takes time to get to know someone."

I know that. But I also know that some people like children and some people don't. And I know that some people are ready and able to be responsive to a child before other people are. All that is fine. But I also know to trust my instincts. My instincts are my direct connection to my inner child. And as a child I learned what it's like to be treated as if you are invisible. I don't like it. It screwed me up. I will not subject my daughter to it.

Damn! I thought everything was going along fine until she met my daughter. But any woman who gets into a relationship with me will also be getting into a relationship with my daughter. We are a package deal.

Maybe this woman is afraid she will have to compete with my daughter for my attention. I should have a sign painted on the back of my jacket saying:

"I have enough love to go around."

I sincerely trust that this is true—that I do. But it doesn't mean my woman friend does.

Need

My dominant feeling at the moment, other than headache, is loneliness. I am travel-weary and sunburned, fearful and anxious, reticent and hesitant—but mostly I am utterly lonely. I haven't felt this lonely in about two or three years. This is not only the loneliness of having no one with you—it is the loneliness of not having a self.

In group therapy a couple of weeks ago, a member commented to me on how terrible it must feel not to have a family. I didn't know what she was talking about, of course, because I have never had the sensation of family. How strange! If I have never had a strong sensation of family, how can I have the strong sensation of not having one? Family is an ancestral, tribal, primordial need.

Celeste is gone for the summer. I am in New York City—utterly, terribly, frighteningly, woundedly, specifically, concretely, bleedingly alone. I am so lonely it has affected my breathing. I am afraid to write for fear of what might come up. I am afraid to stay at home. I am afraid to listen to music because I don't know if I can handle the feelings.

What do I need? What do I crave?

I crave family. Admit it, Dwight, you are a family man without a family. But you've been hurt badly so you are afraid to get involved. But at least I know what I want and I am not afraid to admit it now.

I want to be in love again. I want to build a family. I'm tired of being alone. I want a family. A family. Family.

First Things First

I have been married twice, yet I have never been in an intimate relationship in my life. In all my years of seeking connection with women, I was never looking for intimacy and love. I was looking for the attention I never got as a kid. If a woman threw a morsel of attention my way, then I assumed I was in love with her. I didn't know that, before I could have an intimate relationship with a woman, I had to learn to have an intimate relationship with myself. I was, essentially, trying to walk before I learned how to crawl.

Things have changed. I'm a healthy man. Not a bad catch for a good woman. If I were a woman, I'd go out with me.

I'm going to take my time getting involved again. I'm going to enjoy myself. I am not desperately searching for a woman because I don't want to end up with a desperate woman. I've done that. I've been there. I deserve better than what I have previously allowed myself to become devoted to. I don't want to get involved with what a friend of mine refers to as a BTN—a Better Than Nothing.

Today I reach out in a new and healthier way, so that a new and healthier woman will reach back. I want my daughter to see me in a loving and healthy relationship with a woman. I feel centered and hopeful today. I have grown. I'm proud of myself.

God and My Daughter

I didn't want to teach my daughter how to isolate herself. I didn't want to give her the impression that a person is an entity that exists apart from everything else. My daughter and I have a great relationship, but it takes more than two to make a family. I didn't want her to grow up without a sense of family, or community. I also feel that I am alive and well today by the grace of God, and I wanted to impart some perspective on that spiritual aspect of her father to her.

I went on a church hunt. Nothing seemed right. One day Celeste came out of a Sunday School class with a line drawing of Jesus on the cross with crayon markings smeared madly back and forth across it. That was not what I had in mind for my daughter's spiritual education.

I was about to give up when a friend of mine told me about the Unitarian Church of All Souls here in New York City. One-fifth of the 1,300 member congregation was reportedly in one form of recovery or another. I had also heard of the minister. His name is F. Forrester Church. He is the author of several books. One is *Father and Son,* about his wonderful relationship with his father, the late Sen. Frank Church. This book, of course, made me want to throw up, since I was carrying so much unresolved pain from my relationship with my own father, but it also intrigued me.

I called the church the next day and the first thing I asked was if they had child care. They had a complete church school, for all ages from toddlers to seniors in high school. Bingo! They care about children.

During our first year as members, I went to chapel and Celeste went to church school. She brought home no crayon drawings of Jesus dying on a cross. Instead, she brought home stories of the origin of the Red Cross. She told me about the underground railroad during the Civil War that smuggled black people out of the South to freedom. She told me about famous Unitarians such as Henry David Thoreau and Ralph Waldo Emerson. She talked about the Bible and religious history, not as things to be memorized, but as tools to a greater understanding of peace and love.

The second year of our membership was due to begin in early September. I had never been busier. I was working full time managing a restaurant. I was also in three recovery programs. I was working out three times a week in my gym. I was writing a new book, having just returned from a media tour talking about my first book. And, of course, I was parenting my daughter.

On September first I received a letter from the director of the church school. She asked me if I would be willing to be a teacher there. She said she realized that being a church school teacher was probably the farthest thing from my mind (it was), but she thought I would be a great teacher and a joy to have as a member of the staff.

Neither you nor I could have foreseen, from her simple letter, the impact it would have on me. I began to cry while still holding the letter in my hands. Not only did I have a hard time believing that I was wanted, but it was especially hard for me to believe that I was wanted in such a healthy, wonderful place. This was an invitation to be the leader of a room full of six-year-olds, sitting on little rugs in a circle on the floor of an ivy-covered school adjacent to a beautiful church. This was a sign that I was trusted with the children of the people whose singing trickled through the window of our classroom from the sanctuary next door.

The timing of the invitation to teach was perfect. I was in need of finding a better way to feel connected to my church. I felt a little on the fringe of things, committed but not committed, willing to jump in but not knowing where to get started. This was an opportunity to get involved, to feel good about myself, and to meet people.

I also had the feeling that I wanted another kid, but I didn't even have a girl friend. Slight problem. I specifically asked to teach first grade. I didn't want to be Celeste's second grade teacher. I'm already enough of an authority figure in her life. My request to teach first grade was accepted, and suddenly I had twelve children, yet I had to be with them only once a week. Fun. And not too demanding.

I was brought up without any religion. That had its drawbacks, but it also provided me with a clear blackboard upon which to write my own beliefs. The Unitarian Church encouraged me to do just that. And I, in turn, encouraged the children to do the same.

We began by writing our own classroom covenant. We explained to the children that, in order to have the best possible time together, we needed to agree on a set of rules for ourselves. We asked the children for suggested rules. The rules they offered were amazingly similar to those we adults would have stressed. The kids suggested: no fighting, no speaking out of turn, no stealing each other's tools and toys, and other reasonable and appropriate things. We voted to adopt the rules. Whenever a problem would arise in the classroom, we would ask two questions:

"What are you doing?" and "Is what you are doing following our rules?" We had very few problems with the children.

By teaching the Unitarian purposes and principles to children, I was able to realize and solidify my own religious and spiritual beliefs in simple language. I believe in the importance and value of each person on earth. I believe in a free and fair search for truth and meaning. I believe in a united world, encouraged by an awareness of how we need each other. I believe in stressing our similarities, rather than our differences. I believe in sexual and racial equality. I believe in learning from all religious, scientific, and humanist teachings. I believe in love.

This year I am too busy to teach in the church school. But I am not too busy to worship with my daughter in our church.

Sometimes there are places I would rather be. The same is true for Celeste. But through our association with our liberal religion, we are being encouraged to learn what we believe, rather than being told what to believe. We are being encouraged to ask questions, rather than being stuffed full of pat answers. We are learning to live in the world, without looking out at it. We are discovering what we have in common with all people of the world. We are learning to offer trust and help, and to receive goodness and understanding. It was a pleasure to learn that church is a place to receive, as much as it is a place to give. Church is a place where we have learned to listen, and listened to learn. A lot of the principles that we knew before coming to All Souls have been strengthened. Many new insights and beliefs have been added.

What I see both in my daughter and in myself is the emergence of a strong, yet flexible spiritual self. When we moved closer to God, God, in turn, moved closer to us. Celeste does not gaze upward at some distant deity. Her God is not like some cartoon character with superhuman powers. She has her own understanding of God, which I do not tamper with. When she needs the presence of God, she seems to turn within.

Celeste and I have found for our spirits a home. I am very grateful to our church for helping us to do so.

Asset or Liability?

I used to think that being a single parent was a liability. I thought that I should conceal the fact that I was a single parent until the woman I was on a date with began to like me quite a bit. Then, I imagined, having found me to be a wonderful person, she would tolerate me having a kid.

I soon realized that my attitude said more about me thinking of having a kid as a liability than it said about some imaginary woman I was dating.

I guess, deep within myself, I realize what a difficult job it is to be a parent. I know the thousands of times I have passed up opportunities to do something I really wanted to do because I didn't want to leave my kid or couldn't find a babysitter. I know, intimately, the inability to focus on my work because there is a little runt who looks just like me, standing next to my desk, looking lost and needy. I did not ask to become a parent. It just happened. And I sometimes wonder how a woman could willingly and consciously walk into such a difficult situation.

There is nothing wrong with being a parent and, on occasion, not wanting to be one. After all, I'm a writer and sometimes I wish I wasn't one. I have to take care of my body and sometimes I wish I didn't. Why should something as awesome as parenting be any different?

I must also remember that when I was childless and single, I dated a couple of women with children. I found these women to be deeper, richer in spirit, less pretentious in attitude, and fuller in perspective than most childless women. Come to think of it, I can see similar changes in me since I became a parent. I feel like more of a man, more of a person since I accepted the mission of raising a child. I see people more clearly. I am better able to respond to their needs. Life has become less abstract, more real.

All the old adages can be tested during parenthood. Is it true, for example, that the more you give the more you receive? My daughter, like any infant, was a "need machine," cranking out neediness at an incredible rate. And she was totally devoid of gratitude, like any infant. Yet, ever so strangely, I was filled with love and joy, contentment and compassion, over and over again as I cared for this tiny being. In this way, my daughter has been my greatest teacher. Without uttering a word, without a tooth in her head, making the most awful messes—she inspired me to look deeper and deeper within myself and life itself, until I arrived at a level of understanding that, without her, would have been utterly unreachable.

I cannot imagine living life without a child. And yet I wonder how a woman could be attracted to a single father. How silly. Of course a woman would be attracted to a single father! I am a man firmly planted within the soil of my own humanity. And I owe so much of it to a little girl who looks just like me. Funny how at times a child can look like a liability, and at others can become your greatest teacher.

Blessed with Addiction

It is because of—and not in spite of—my addiction that I have become the person I am today. My addiction was my greatest teacher. If, with a magic wand I could have could have eliminated my greatest curse, alcoholism, I might have been a perfect baby. But who needs perfect babies in a perfect world? Because by removing my greatest curse, alcoholism, I would also have removed my greatest blessing. This is not to say that I think everyone should be afflicted with alcoholism so that they can experience the thrill of recovery from it!

What I am saying is that I am firmly convinced that my life today is better than it might have been had I not been defeated by alcohol and drugs. I was involved in a fierce fight with booze and pills. I lost. When I admitted that I lost, I won. Because of my addiction, I learned the incredible spiritual lesson of victory through surrender. I learned that it was through acceptance, not fighting or rage or repulsion, that change comes.

Defeated in my attempts to be someone I wasn't, I became able to learn, love, and accept myself for who I am. By letting go of my grip on the past, my hands were free to embrace the future.

I am thirty-nine years old and ten years clean and sober. After a period of mourning my lost years, I began to experience and nurture myself as a creative human being again. I am writing, living, and loving better than ever. My pre-recovery writing seems two-dimensional to me now, as if I were viewing life through a periscope sticking up from the bottom of a glass of brandy. Now my lens is wide open. Recovery from addiction unburied a love of life I didn't know was there.

There are many things that could happen to my daughter in the course of her life, and alcoholism is one of them. I cannot protect her from destiny or chance. I can hope to God that my daughter does not become an active alcoholic, and go through the hell that her father somehow survived. Celeste is only nine, but she has been aware of the family disease for over four years. When asked recently at a dinner party if she wanted to try a sip of wine, she replied, "No, thank you. There is alcoholism in the family and I might be allergic."

My daughter also has been blessed by my defeat. What I have done is to take the spiritual lessons that recovery afforded me, and apply them to the challenge of parenting. Should alcoholism afflict her, the love and nurturing she is receiving as a child, coupled with her awareness of the family disease, will, I hope, free her from the supposed certainty of predisposition to addiction. My recovery might provide her with a choice.

There are worse things that could happen to you than to have a treatable disease in the family. The disease of alcoholism was potentially my escape hatch, but ultimately it proved to be my port of entry into the world.

A Sense of Self

As usual, Celeste and I were having an impossible time getting ready for school. She came out of her bedroom wearing a gold sweater and purple pants.

"I look terrible," she said.

"No, you don't," I replied, telling the truth, but also mindful of already being late, and dreading another change of clothes by a nine-year-old who couldn't make up her mind. She could have had chocolate pudding smeared all over her body and I would have said it looked terrific.

"I look terrible," she repeated.

"No, you don't," I repeated more emphatically. "The Minnesota Vikings are a famous football team and their official colors are (I think) gold and purple. And remember Dad telling you about Mardi Gras? Their official colors are gold and purple. EVERYONE knows that gold and purple go together."

"No, they don't."

I have been Celeste's father long enough to know that I cannot win in this situation. I gave up and allowed her to rifle through her wardrobe, which she seemed to feel was specifically designed to not look right. Years later, or so it seemed, she emerged from her room wearing the same purple pants, but with a funky old tee shirt that was clearly (to me) not going to be warm enough. I struck a deal with her that she would carry the gold sweater in her backpack just in case she got cold. She reluctantly agreed.

A few minutes later I fired off a one-line verbal zinger at her. It was nothing terrible, vulgar, or hateful. I don't even remember the words. I just remember feeling that, if what I had just said to my daughter had been said to me when I was a kid, it would have gotten through my defenses, and I would have carried around the pain for a long time. I didn't even have time to feel guilty about what I had said before Celeste, without looking up from the cereal she was eating, said to me, "You're trying to hurt me. It isn't going to work."

I looked at my little sweetie, who was wearing a baseball cap and shoveling corn flakes into her mouth, and I chuckled.

"Good for you," I said to her. "Good for you."

I got her to school, not nearly as late as I had feared, and just before we parted I said to her, "You can be kinda stubborn, can't you?"

"Yup," she replied.

Later that day I reviewed all that had happened. I realized I had been doing some things I didn't like but felt incapable of stopping. First of all, I was trying to impose my taste in clothing upon my daughter. Where did I get the notion that my taste in clothing is better than my daughter's? Whatever happened to 'beauty is in the eye of the beholder'? Second, why did I say something to my daughter in hopes of hurting her? I really don't know. I am entitled to be a jerk sometimes and to make mistakes.

What really interests me is my daughter's response. She was not about to let me tell her what to wear. She intuitively knew that what she liked had nothing to do with what pleased me. The fact that I didn't understand was clearly my problem.

I was so proud of Celeste when she said, "You're trying to hurt me. It isn't going to work." She was perceptive enough to hear what I was REALLY saying, and to detect my motive. She refused to let my negativity affect her on a deep level. When I laughed and said, "Good for you," she knew that I was affirming her independence of spirit, in accordance with everything I have taught her, even though she had used the lesson "against" me. Wow! An nine-year-old girl is confronted with the anger, disapproval, and manipulation of her father, whom she loves very much, and she still stands her ground!

I am confident that Celeste, as an adult, will be able to deal with big issues like alcoholism and loss. But she will also be able to deal with issues that are important, but not life-threatening. For example, the little girl who says to her father, "You're trying to hurt me—it isn't going to work," will most likely become a woman who is not about to compromise herself in order to secure the approval of others. I marvel at the way she moves through life with her head held high, feeling like a valuable member of the human race.

Celeste reminds me of what I might have been like without the ravages of addiction and madness that stalked my self-esteem from childhood on. I too was a strong person with a strong sense of self. But, as the steady application of tiny drops of water will eventually turn a rock into a pebble, the steady application of abuse whittled me down to almost nothing.

People like me often wonder if this phenomenon of self-help groups, weekend retreats, recovery books, massage therapy, spirituality seminars, health clubs, special diets, and on and on really works. Sometimes it's hard to tell. Often I will deny or distort the results. For example, if I invest enough time or money in something, I will convince myself it is working even if it clearly isn't.

But you can't pretend like that with a child. You can be reading a self-help book, but if your child is off, lost, staring into his or her soup, you know you have a problem. Celeste is the evidence to me that, no matter how you were treated as a child, with hard work, good luck, and intuition, you can parent a child the way you were never parented.

The process of recovery results in changed behavior. How much more beautiful and hopeful an ending could I have than this? I have been granted a life worth waiting for. I have let go of my old ways of dealing with the world. I have forgiven my parents and moved on to a new life. I have in my life now a small child who is the hope of her ancestors and a beacon of light at the dawning of a new generation of freedom.

Happy Mother's Day to Me

Today is Mother's Day. I got a Mother's Day card from a friend of mine. The card mentions all sorts of wonderful things that a good mother is. My friend, who is a single parent with three children, figured that since I fit the bill so well, I must be a mother. She wrote in the card:

Dear Dwight,
I thought this card
was very descriptive
of the wonderful "mothering"
I know you do.
Love,
Kris

    She is right. I am a good mother. It is kind of too bad that loving and nurturing, packing a lunch box, and braiding hair have come to be known as woman's work. But I know better. These things are the work of a loving parent, no matter what the gender.
    I am proud of being a Daddymom. There are many, many times when I do something with my daughter and I am the only male parent in the room. That sometimes hurts. I sometimes feel lonely. But I don't let these feelings get in the way of my parenting.
    My daughter knows nothing about jobs in the home breaking down along sexual lines. For her it is easy: I do everything and she watches! She collects baseball cards and I wear rubber gloves to protect my hands when I do the dishes.
    It's not that I think there are no differences between the sexes. There are. But they don't rule me. Flexibility is the trick. My daughter has been with me on Mother's Day for the

last six years. And she is with me on Father's Day too. Being a single parent who refuses to be dominated by all the confusing rules and roles has it's benefits. I get to celebrate more holidays.

Happy Mother's Day to all the mothers—no matter what sex they are!

Fruitcake

Welcome to parenthood. You get to become everything you hated in your parents. You get to hear yourself mouthing trite little ditties about what will happen to your child when and if the child does or doesn't do the things you did or didn't do when you were his or her age. Your parents told you the same things you are now telling your kid. You didn't listen, and yet you turned out fine. Nobody listens to this stuff. It just keeps going around and around like an unopened fruitcake being passed from relative to relative. No one uses it, but no one throws it away either.

When I was a kid I had a friend whose mother strapped raw pieces of potato to his forehead to cure his headache. It worked. But then, I don't have any warts on my hands, when, by all accounts, I should be covered with them from handling frogs.

So who got caught holding the fruitcake today? And who has a watermelon growing in the stomach because of swallowing one of the seeds?

Parenting is crazy business, done by people who pretend to know what they are doing for the sake of the kids. My secret to good parenting is simple: Do the best you can and hope for the best results.

Check the Spelling

Celeste and I were riding our bikes through Central Park on our way to school when she turned to me and said, "My friend Ethan and I were in school the other day and we were writing a story on the computer. The teacher said everything was very good except the spelling and now I am thinking that it would be really neat if computers had a button you could push and it would check the spelling on all the words."

"They already do have something like that, Celeste. It is called Spell Check."

"I knew that," she blurted out before I had even completed my sentence.

"Does it bother you that somebody already thought of it?"

"Of course not."

"Good. Because I'll tell you something, Celeste. There are tons of grown-up men and women, at this very minute, who are working in fancy computer offices, making lots and lots of money, trying to come up with ideas as good as what this little girl named Celeste just came up with all on her own. I'm very proud of you, Celeste. You have a very creative mind. I like the way you think. And I have a feeling that, sooner or later, you are going to think of something that no one else in the world has thought of. In the meantime, don't be too disappointed that someone thought of this one thing before you did."

"Well, I was a little bit disappointed. But now that you talked to me, I feel better."

"I feel better too, Celeste."

Hiccups

I was putting Celeste to bed last night and, somehow, the conversation turned to magic.

"I'm magic," I said to her.

"You are not," she said.

"Oh, yes I am," I exclaimed.

"Prove it to me," she said defiantly.

"Okay. Within ten minutes you will begin to hiccup," I said, as I squiggled my fingers around and said "abracadabra!"

Two minutes later Celeste began to hiccup. I started laughing and so did she. "I told you I was magic," I said as I laughed.

"No, you're not. Do one more thing," she pleaded as she hiccuped.

"No. One is enough. The next one will cost you five dollars," I said.

"No. Do one more! One more! The last one was coincidence," she said, getting a little irritated with my refusal to admit that it had been just dumb luck.

"Okay! Okay! I'll do just one more. You will stop hiccuping within the next five minutes. Abracadabra!" I said as I once again squiggled my fingers around in some meaningless manner designed to make me look like a sorcerer casting spells.

"I'm going to go get you some water for your night stand," I said to her.

"No! I know that water makes hiccups go away!" Celeste shouted to me.

"Okay. Forget it. No water," I said.

"Hey!" Celeste said with a look of surprise on her face, "the hiccups are gone!"

This time I joined Celeste in thinking that this wasn't funny. We didn't talk much about it that night. Celeste acted like she had just experienced something a little bit spooky. I tucked her in. She went to sleep muttering something about me not being magic, no matter what I did. I agreed with her.

When I went to bed a while later, I remembered how, as a child, and even as a young adult, I was afraid of and tried to deny my power. My father was a very powerful man. My mother had terrific telepathic powers. And both of them were raging alcoholics. My mother used her telepathic powers to intrude on people. She was a sort of spiritual Peeping Tom. My father used his powers to hurt people. He had a lot of evil in him, and used his power to whittle away at people. For example, he had the uncanny ability to anticipate people's responses to what he was about to say. He was able to, in effect, see into the future. He used that ability to defeat and manipulate people.

If I have indeed inherited some of my parents' power, should I be afraid of it, for fear that power is in and of itself evil? Just as I was, as a child, afraid of anger because it always led to violence, I have been, as an adult, afraid of power because I thought it always led to struggle, manipulation, and evil.

But just because I am afraid of my power doesn't mean it isn't there. A couple of months ago I was speaking on the phone with a friend. I was in my apartment. She was in hers. As we spoke on the phone, I accurately described the room she was sitting in to her. I had never been in her apartment before. She called today when I was writing this and I told her about the hiccups. She reminded me about how I described her apartment without having ever seen it. I had forgotten about that. Or, more accurately, I had denied it had ever happened.

My life today is about accepting who I am. I must learn to accept my faults, as well as my assets. I must learn to accept the body I live in and its limitations. I must also learn to accept the expansiveness of the potent spiritual force that passes through and empowers me. I am awash with energy. To gain its benefits, I don't even have to work at it. All I have to do is to learn how to tap into the vast reserves of energy and spirituality available to me. The main way to do that is to remain a clean and clear conductor of the power. And I must learn not to fear it any longer.

Maybe my daughter's hiccups—and their cure—were coincidental. Maybe they weren't. Whatever the case, I will be open to the possibility of power. This time, instead of running from it because of its potential for abuse, I will bow to and embrace whatever power is within me as a tool for the body and a balm for the spirit.

I am much more powerful than I think. When I take a deep breath, a universe fills my chest. I live in a large, large world. I used to work so hard to keep my world small, manageable, and boring. But now I want to realize and accept my power. I pray that I will use my gift wisely and humbly. Then I need not fear that which God has freely given me. Even if it is just a case of the hiccups.

What It Takes

She was cranky. I could tell she had that creepy feeling, the spiritual equivalent of not being able to brush your teeth or wash your hair because you have been traveling. She was squirmy and uncomfortable. She was looking for a fight with me and trashed all my attempts at finding out what was wrong. She didn't know what was wrong any more than I did. She was grumpily getting ready for school. I was coldly ignoring her and getting ready for work.

We passed each other in the hallway. I intentionally stood in her way. Celeste is a lovely little girl, but I hate to mess with her. She has inherited my stubborn disposition, and won't give up the fight. She glared up at me. I froze like a deer on a highway at night that had just been doused in headlights. I awaited the horrible consequences of getting in the way of "the kid."

I had no idea that I was going to say anything, and I don't know where the inspiration came from, but I found myself the proud inheritor of the following words:

"Celeste, I have to do something now. I hope you can learn to forgive me. But, you see, I just can't help it."

With that declaration out of the way, I picked her up and held her gently. She wasn't crazy about it at first, and kept her arms tightly at her sides, waiting for the disgusting hug to be over. I didn't say a word. I just held her gently, and swayed slightly from side to side. Eventually, like an ice cube floating around in a glass of tap water, she began to melt. She actually felt lighter, and softer. She breathed slowly. Her cheek was pressed against mine, and I felt her jaws unclench. Her face became flushed and warm. She surrendered to the love.

I gave her a little kiss on the cheek, and put her down. She went into her room. I could hear her humming as she was putting on her shoes. And then we left for school.

Celestial

You are perfect. The color of your hair. The shape of your eyes. Your insatiable appetite for learning. Your willingness to ask for what you need. I think you are the best thing since the invention of spaghetti.

You are getting older. Once you were my baby and you looked to me for everything. Now you are tall and sturdy. You think you own the world. Sometimes I'm inclined to agree. The world is a place you are comfortable in. Keep it that way. No self-doubt. Firm, yet flexible opinions. So self-assured.

Amazing how many different emotions can sweep across you in a matter of moments. You can go from anger to love to sadness to fatigue to testy to pensive. Tears can fall into the corner of your smile. And there is nothing suspicious or contradictory about that. No one tells you that you are schizophrenic or confused or unable to make up your mind. You simply have access to the full spectrum of your emotional self. That means you know how to feel all your feelings as soon as they happen within you. What a blessing. What a wonderful thing for me to learn from you.

Share Me

Just because Celeste wants me to get a girl friend who will also serve as a mother figure in her life doesn't necessarily mean that Celeste wants me to get a girl friend who will also serve as a mother figure in her life.

In other words, just because she wants it doesn't mean she wants it. Celeste sees no contradiction in having opposite feelings occur in her simultaneously. She wants me to have a relationship with a woman so that I won't be lonely and so that she can develop her own relationship with that woman. But Celeste also wants me all to herself.

That makes perfect sense to me. I never learned to compromise or to share. I never thought there was enough love to go around. It was either me or you who got the love, the attention, the nurturing. And if you got it instead of me, it felt as if you stole it from me. I deserved it, but you got it. Not fair.

As a kid, this ruthless aggression was born in me. I had to get there first and take it all, even if I didn't want it. I would hide a cola under my mattress, restless all night on the lump it created, in order to drink it alone, warm and overly bubbly, in a dark closet the following day. It tasted awful, but if I had left it in the refrigerator it would have been yours. Youngest child. Not enough to go around. Got to move fast. Nice guys come in last.

Sharing the things you love most in life doesn't make sense to a child. Civility is an acquired taste. A prerequisite for it is a healthy sense of self. If you are raised with a fear of emotional or physical abandonment, you are going to grow up and be called greedy, when, in fact, you're really only needy.

Just how loving am I? How strong is my sense of balance? What is required of me to move toward my new friend without it appearing that I am turning my back on Celeste? Just how capable of love is the woman I am dating? How strong is her sense of self? Will she feel that she must compete fiercely with an nine-year-old girl for my attention?

Trust cannot exist without a sense of safety. Feeling safe is achieved when you believe that your needs will be met. Believing your needs will be met is achieved by being loved in a consistent and appropriate manner.

I have loved Celeste to the best of my ability every day of her life. Even on days when I feel unloving and unlovable, there is always a huge reservoir of love that I can tap into. Love, like electricity or sound waves, fills the spaces between us at all times. I have to bypass love in order to become unloving.

When Celeste sees that I don't have just this tiny morsel of love, like a crust of bread, to share amongst three people—when she sees that, strangely enough, it is by giving away love that I guarantee the infinite supply of love—when she sees that the way to save is to expend—then she will know there is enough love to go around. Love need not be feared or hoarded. The more I love, the more lovable I become. It will be my actions, more than my words, that will illustrate to Celeste that loving a woman will make me a better father.

Parenting in Recovery

I have hope that, because of the work I am doing in recovery, the closest my daughter will ever come to the kind of abuse I knew as a child will be to read a book about it.

My daughter will not be able to identify emotionally with some of the relationship issues her father has: fear of intimacy, terminal shyness, stuffing feelings. These are absent in her character.

Celeste is a different person than I am. I have seen her scratch her head in loving puzzlement about what life must have been like growing up in a home troubled by addiction and abuse. She can't relate to being raised in a dysfunctional family. Amazing.

I have met men and women in recovery who are afraid to have children. They fear that they might do to their own child what was done to them. But I also see many, many men and women in recovery who are learning how to have intimate relationships in spite of the way they were raised. These people are learning how to love.

That very love is the sustenance of our future generations.

About the Author

Dwight Lee Wolter, poet, journalist, and lecturer, is the author of two other acclaimed books, *A Life Worth Waiting For!* and *Forgiving Our Parents* (both from CompCare Publishers). His books have been reviewed by the *New York Times,* the *Los Angeles Times, American Health* magazine, and many other magazines and newspapers. He has been interviewed on over 100 radio stations, including national public radio's "New Dimensions," and has appeared on "Geraldo" and CBS "This Morning." He and his daughter were the subject of an "NBC Nightly News" feature on children of alcoholics and were interviewed by Barbara Walters for an ABC special on genetic engineering. Two of his audiotapes, *Forgiving Our Parents* and *Sex and Celibacy,* have been released by Recovery Resource Group/Listen to Learn Tape Library.

He gives presentations and conducts workshops nationally on dysfunctional families, men's issues, parenting, and forgiveness. He was a keynote speaker at a National Council on Alcoholism and Drug Dependency (NCADD) and is a consultant to treatment centers on men's issues.

Dwight Wolter lives in New York City with his young daughter, Celeste.

Dwight Lee Wolter can be contacted for presentations and workshops by calling CompCare Publishers' national toll-free number, 800/328-3330, or in Minnesota 612/559-4800.

Resource List of Topics

Abandonment, fear of, 53-60
Acceptance, 35
Addiction, as a positive force, 160-161
Angels, guardian, 131-132
Anger, expressing, 38-41, 127-129
Behavior, healthy vs. dysfunctional, 116-121
Being alone, 55-60
Blame, shifting, 124-126
Boundaries, emotional and physical, 8
Caught between parents, 116-122, 137-144
Change and growth, 49-50
Childlike vision, 22-23
Child relationships, 72-73
Children as teachers, 158-159
Compliance, 53-60
Control, parents', 31-32, 38-41
Death, explaining and coping with, 70-71, 97-108
Disappointment, 168
Divorce, 24
Dysfunctional childhood, effects of, 26-29, 32, 95-96, 103-105, 132, 169-171
Dysfunctional parenting, 163-164
Fairness, 20-21
Family, meaning of, 61-66
Family, need for, 152
Fear of loss, 67-68
Fear, overcoming, 74-78
Feelings, expressing, 11, 13-15, 173, 69
Flexibility, 31-32
Forgiveness, 116-123

Giving in to a child's demands, 38-41
Grieving with a child, 106-108
Guilt, a child's, 13-15
Guilt, a parent's, 127-129, 47-48
Growth milestones, 33-34, 36-37
Growth through pain, 124-126, 127-129
Help, asking for, 30, 146-149
Illness, 95-96, 93-94
Insecurity, 42-43
Intuition, listening to, 12
Learning to love, 95-96, 122-123
Learning to say no, 53-56
Letting go, 137-145, 67-68
Listening to God, 79-84
Loneliness, 87-92, 152
Love, 172, 176
Money, value of, 51-52
Parenting, good, 14-15
Parenting, joys of, 6
"Perfect" parent, 9-10
Perfectionism, 11
Power, fear of, 169-171
Power, limits to, 35
Power of parents, 45-46
Prayer for help, 57-59
Preserving a child's dreams, 130-133
Regrets, 1-2
Religion, parenting and, 154-157
Repressing feelings, 69
Responsibility, 7
Risk-taking, 74-78
Self-acceptance, 136-137

Self-blame, 87-92
Self-doubt, 113-115
Self-love, 153
Self-parenting, 26-29
Separation anxiety, 53-60, 62-66, 137-145
Sex, discussing, 44
Shame, letting go of, 47-48
Sharing, 174-175
Single parenting and dating, 150-151, 158-159
Single parenting, difficulties and rewards, 1-3, 4-5, 93-94, 158-159
Single parenting, fears, 53-60
Single parenting, absence of sex roles, 165-166
Spirituality, finding one's, 154-157
Stepparent, accepting your child's, 137-145
Subjugating one's needs, 66, 90-92
Understanding children, 17-18
Verbal abuse, 38-41
Victim guilt, 146-149
Wishes, 16